Peter ONE

A Modern Day Commentary on First Peter

By
Mel Reed

Optimus Training Publications
Fayetteville, AR 72704

Also by Mel Reed
James & I & YOU
NFL-Never Fail Leadership
365-QUEST for MEN

Peter ONE
A Modern Day Commentary on First Peter
By Mel Reed

ISBN: 978-0-9894341-0-2

Optimus Training Publications
Fayetteville, Arkansas 72704

Library of Congress Control Number: 2014910746

Copyright 2014 by Mel Reed-Optimus Training

Cover Art: Gerrit van Honthorst (Utrecht 1590-1656)

All rights reserved. No part of this book may be reproduced without written permission from the publisher or copyright holder, except in the case of brief quotations embodied in critical articles and reviews.
No part of this book may be transmitted in any form or by any means- electronically, mechanically, photocopied, recorded, or other-means without prior written permission from the publisher or copyright holder.

Unless otherwise indicated, Scripture taken from the HOLY BIBLE, NEW INTERNATIONAL VERSION. Copyright© 1973,1978,1984 International Bible Society. Used by permission of Zondervan Bible Publishers. All right reserved worldwide. http://www.zondervan.com

Peter ONE

PREFACE

Do you love me? Then Feed my Sheep. Can you hear Jesus, asking you that same question today? If so, what is your answer?

What does it mean to be a Christian? And are we any different from the rest of society? The apostle Peter wrote a letter to a group of early Christians to encourage and to assist them in understanding the answer to those questions.

First Peter the epistle written by Simon Peter, the apostle and disciple that walked with, ate with, and learned from Jesus. In this short but powerful letter, he helps the reader understand what happens when they are converted, and how to walk out this life here on earth as a follower of Christ.

This is a modern day commentary, a journey through this timely and powerful writing from the New Testament. First Peter tackles subjects like, Holiness, Submission, and Suffering. In this "entertain me now" world, it is actually refreshing to drink from Gods word, and satisfy the thirst for truth. Come drink and walk in FREEDOM , for this world cannot offer the truth that sets men free.

Peter One, will help you embrace your position in Christ and challenge you to live in the freedom of God, even when all Hell is breaking out against you trying to destroy your faith.

Peter ONE

1 Peter

1:1 Peter, an apostle of Jesus Christ,

To God's elect, exiles scattered throughout the provinces of Pontus, Galatia, Cappadocia, Asia and Bithynia,

1:2 who have been chosen according to the foreknowledge of God the Father, through the sanctifying work of the Spirit, to be obedient to Jesus Christ and sprinkled with his blood:

Grace and peace be yours in abundance.

It is sure that the author of this letter is Peter. There is debate surrounding who wrote many of the other works of the Bible, but here, as we begin our walk through this first epistle of Peter, let's pray that truth be revealed line by line, verse by verse. Sound reasonable? His name was Simon, but Jesus changed it to Peter (John 1:42). Why would Jesus do that? Simon is a perfectly good name, and if you look up its meaning it will read, "From the Hebrew name *Shim'on,* which meant *he has heard."* So why go from "he has heard" to a name meaning "rock or stone?" There has been much discussion over the centuries, and if you are a curious sort there are volumes written regarding the subject. That is not the purpose of our focus. It is an interesting study, though, if you ever get the urge to seek it out.

Peter ONE

A few years back, I led a men's retreat on the edge of a lake – one of the exercises during the weekend was to ask God to reveal to each man God's "name" for them.

You see, it is easy for us to accept our name – you know, the one our parents had recorded on our birth certificate. But what if God has another name for you? What if that name speaks of new character, higher purpose, and constantly reminds you of the call?

Simon became Peter, Saul became Paul, Abram became Abraham – so it may not be such a wild idea to at least listen and see. Read the first chapter of Luke, regarding the birth of John the Baptist. God named this baby boy John, or we would have had Zechariah the Baptist! God sent angels to Elizabeth and Mary to make sure these cousins were named John and Jesus. He had a purpose and a plan for each. And God has a plan and purpose for you.

During our retreat, there were no angelic visitations to my knowledge, but several men prayed it through and discovered God's special name for themselves. They were given a "new" name that spoke to their heart, given to them by the Father. Have you ever had a family member tag you with a less-than-flattering nickname? You know, the kind that every time you hear it, it makes you cringe? That is not what we are talking about here. But, when someone you love calls you that special name, the name that makes you feel strong and closer, it builds you up from the inside out. The apostles had a special name for a guy in the early church. (read Acts 4:36)

Peter ONE

Remember a guy named Joseph, a Levite from Cyprus? Probably not, you most likely know him as "Barnabas", which means *Son of Encouragement*.

Here in our text, Simon becomes Peter. Otherwise, we would be walking through First Simon together. In the opening remarks of this letter, he refers to himself as an Apostle of Jesus Christ. In those days, most letters started with a greeting of sorts, something clarifying, stating who was holding the pen and to whom the letter was being written. I call this the "*I Am – You Are*" statement.

Peter made sure to greet his readers, who were followers of Christ. The letter was written about 30 years after Jesus's ascension, following his resurrection. And here we are – many centuries later – reading these words together as Christians, Followers of Christ.

Peter, an Apostle of Christ, wrote to us, who have been chosen. We who have been chosen by whom?

Well, the answer to that question is found in verse two. He mentions the Father, the Son, and the Holy Spirit. The Holy Trinity, God in three persons, chose us. Think on it: we have been called into relationship with the creator of the universe, to personally walk with him, talk with him, and follow him! It is only through the blood of Christ that we enter into this new and everlasting covenant. Peter then asks that *"grace and peace be ours, in abundance."*

Peter ONE

The theme of the Old Testament was obedience and sacrifice. But Christ died on the cross as the once-and-for-all sacrifice for man. So, the New Testament themes are obedience, grace, and mercy. Peter's words ring true: we are saved by grace. Thank God! This world is not our home; we were never meant to accept this place, Earth, as the most important place in our minds or hearts. Yet, some walk as though earthly gains are somehow redeeming in themselves. This world has little to offer once you have seen and tasted the goodness of the Lord. If Christ is your Savior as he is mine, we have been restored back to God the Father.

Praise to God for a Living Hope

1:3 Praise be to the God and Father of our Lord Jesus Christ! In his great mercy he has given us new birth into a living hope through the resurrection of Jesus Christ from the dead.

1:4 and into an inheritance that can never perish, spoil or fade. This inheritance is kept in heaven for you...

In the NIV version of the Bible, there are 313 exclamation points. Verse 3 happens to hold one of them. It is placed immediately following "Jesus Christ," as if to say, "This is who warrants your praise!"

Peter mentions the God and Father of our Lord Jesus Christ! We must remember that they are one and the same.

Peter ONE

Jesus, in **John 10:30,** said, *"I and the Father are one."*

Through the years I have developed this attitude of communication. I pray to God *through* and *in* the name of Jesus, being led by the Holy Spirit. Maybe we say, "Praise Be to God," or, "Praise the Lord," to encourage each other. Or perhaps you have never praised God or uttered those words out loud. It is never too late. Say it with me,

"Father God, in the name of Jesus, and through the power of the Holy Spirit, I thank you for your great love. I praise you and you alone, for you are mighty and wonderful."

Peter writes, "Praise be to the 'God and Father,'" and then he uses the full title of our "Lord Jesus Christ." Think about it: "Lord" acknowledges his complete authority, "Jesus" (*"God saves"*) acknowledges his human name given by Mary and Joseph under the direction of an angel, and then "Christ" (*"Messiah"*) acknowledges his role. Peter wrote this letter in Greek, not in Hebrew, which meant that it would be delivered to the Gentiles to be read and reread easily. So when he says, "Praise be to God," we read it with an anticipating heart and spirit.

Have you ever been to a place on Earth that just took your breath away? Maybe it was a beautiful beach with white sand and emerald water, with a warm breeze swaying through the palm trees. Maybe it was a snow-covered mountaintop in the Rockies or the Alps, where the air was so crisp you could almost taste it.

Peter ONE

Sometimes we become so familiar with our surroundings that we lose our sense of awe regarding them. Some people who live close to these special places become numb to the beauty of their surroundings.

That's what it is like being a follower of Christ. Sometimes, we are so loved and so comfortable that we become complacent. I think we need to remember on a daily basis that we serve an awesome God who deserves all our praise, all our honor, and all our hearts. We need to praise the living God, whose great mercy not only has given us new life but also gives us new breath every moment of every day. Go ahead and remember the depths of despair and sin from which you were once delivered by Christ. The freedom you knew on that day took your breath away. Let the redeeming grace that none of us deserves fill your heart and renew an upright spirit within you.

Over the years, the term "born again" has been made into religious terminology. In reality, it is a loving relationship statement that produces so much awe that we realize our current breath, our last, and our next are all due to the creator whose great love compels us forward.

We are saved, converted, and born again when we accept this Lord Jesus Christ as the Savior of the world, and our personal Savior and when we accept that we are his. His grace and mercy restores living hope within us.

Peter ONE

Then, Peter goes on to say that in him we have *"an inheritance that can never perish, spoil, or fade."*

Then he writes that this inheritance is *"kept in Heaven for you."* What does that mean? There is more? Yes, there's more – it's like one of those late-night ads on TV that sells knives! They are the best knives ever for only $19.99… but, wait, there's more! If you order today, we will double the order! But, wait, there's more! As believers, we can have victory here in this life. As we pray to Father God that his will be done on Earth as it is in Heaven, we can experience some heaven on earth. Just wait… there's more!…*An inheritance that will not fade or perish, kept in heaven for you!*

What a wonderful God we serve – we thank him for his grace and mercy. There is always more when you allow your heart to ponder the wonderful secrets of God.

1:5 who through faith are shielded by God's power until the coming of the salvation that is ready to be revealed in the last time.

Here, Peter encourages the Christians of that day and today to trust in the Lord. This Peter – the one who walked with Jesus, broke bread with the Savior, prayed with the very Son of God, and saw miracle after miracle. Yet, Peter still denied our Lord when the heat was on. Three times, he said he never knew this Jesus. Read the account in **Luke 22:54-62** and in **Matthew 26:69-75**.

Peter ONE

Matthew 26:69-75- *Peter Disowns Jesus*

⁶⁹ Now Peter was sitting out in the courtyard, and a servant girl came to him. "You also were with Jesus of Galilee," she said.

⁷⁰ But he denied it before them all. "I don't know what you're talking about," he said.

⁷¹ Then he went out to the gateway, where another servant girl saw him and said to the people there, "This fellow was with Jesus of Nazareth."

⁷² He denied it again, with an oath: "I don't know the man!"

⁷³ After a little while, those standing there went up to Peter and said, "Surely you are one of them; your accent gives you away."

⁷⁴ Then he began to call down curses, and he swore to them, "I don't know the man!"

Immediately a rooster crowed. ⁷⁵ Then Peter remembered the word Jesus had spoken: "Before the rooster crows, you will disown me three times." And he went outside and wept bitterly."

Peter knew the guilt and shame of denial. But he also knew the joy of forgiveness and restoration. In Mark 16 we read of the account of the Resurrection of Christ.

Peter ONE

Mark 16:1 - *The Resurrection*

When the Sabbath was over, Mary Magdalene, Mary the mother of James, and Salome bought spices so that they might go to anoint Jesus' body.

The earliest the women could go to the tomb and properly embalm the body of Jesus was on Sunday morning. Sabbath was over at the start of Saturday evening, but it wasn't light enough until Sunday morning to do the work.

[6] *"Don't be alarmed," he said. "You are looking for Jesus the Nazarene, who was crucified. He has risen! He is not here. See the place where they laid him.* [7] *But go, tell his disciples and Peter, 'He is going ahead of you into Galilee. There you will see him, just as he told you.'*

Is it not amazing that Jesus sent an angel to deliver the message that he wanted to meet with these men who failed Him in their human weakness, and He makes special note of Peter. *"Tell his disciples, and Peter"...* Does he distinguish Peter here because he is *separate* from the rest of the disciples in the sense that he is no longer among them? Or is it Jesus distinguished Peter because He had special hope, special forgiveness, and special restoration just for Peter?

Jesus, after his resurrection, appeared to his Disciples – even to Thomas, who was called Didymus, the doubter. See, another name change! Jesus appeared early in the morning by the Sea of Tiberias, where he made

The Other Guy who Walked on Water!

Peter ONE

breakfast for some of the disciples, including Simon Peter.

Let's pick up the story in **John 21:15-17**

John 21:15-17- Jesus Reinstates Peter

15 When they had finished eating, Jesus said to Simon Peter, "Simon son of John, do you love me more than these?"

"Yes, Lord," he said, "you know that I love you."

Jesus said, "Feed my lambs."

16 Again Jesus said, "Simon son of John, do you love me?"

He answered, "Yes, Lord, you know that I love you."

Jesus said, "Take care of my sheep."

17 The third time he said to him, "Simon son of John, do you love me?"

Peter was hurt because Jesus asked him the third time, "Do you love me?" He said, "Lord, you know all things; you know that I love you."

Jesus said, "Feed my sheep."

See the sequence of the reinstatement?

Peter ONE

Feed my lambs, take care of my sheep, and feed my sheep

I read this story not just as the reinstatement of Peter, but as the restoration of a man who messed up. He was afraid. Fear caused him to turn his back on his friend, his Savior, and to deny Christ three times. After the work on the cross, though, Jesus had Peter confess his love for Christ three times, and he tells him,
"Feed my lambs, feed my sheep, and take care of my sheep."

The Good Shepherd passing on his shepherding responsibilities to Peter is a lesson for all of us. Feed the lambs; feed the new believers. Feed the sheep; the flock needs the food of truth from the Word of God. Then, he says to *"care"* for the sheep. Do not just feed them, but *care* for the flock. Feed the sheep, give them the truth, and then care for them and help make disciples of converts. Jesus said, *"The sheep that I call, they know my voice."*

Peter, at that point, stood broken and contrite. He was being validated and called all over again. He was called back into fellowship with the Master. He was given an assignment to continue in the ministry, and he must have been elated to know he would be a part of moving the Kingdom of God forward.

Through the generations, many people have experienced this same type of forgiveness. I am one. I denied my Lord through ignorance, and I have disobeyed Him. Once I came to my senses, I knew what

Peter ONE

I had done, and through it all He loved me enough to forgive me. Jesus will allow us to feed his sheep, to love his lambs, and to care for others, even after we have messed up. So, my encouragement is to seek after the Christ, no matter how checkered your past may be.

The letter we are reading was written some 30 years after these events; even after the passage of time, we see a man still full of hope. We know he has hope when he writes of *"the coming salvation that is ready to be revealed in the last time."*

Peter encourages us to trust God until Jesus comes again. The Apostles saw Jesus go back to Heaven. They heard the angels say that Jesus would return, and through the generations since then, many have thought it would happen in their lifetime. The truth is that no one knows the time that the Son of God, Jesus, will return except for God the Father, but this promise has encouraged people throughout history. Stop and look around today: is anyone talking about Jesus coming back today?

Some people in the world want to put him back in the tomb, in that dark place where the Light of the World lay. There, the Son of God was wrapped in the grave clothes, silenced. They want to shut this Savior up! They want to ignore his loving demands for a better way to live and love for all of mankind. They want him out of the way so they can live any way they want. Sin is still sin, even if no one around calls it sin.

Peter ONE

Yes, the Truth that gives so many hope is the same Truth that condemns many to their own dark place. Sadly, many in the world today still walk in the darkness, and they want to put Jesus back in the dark tomb. To them I declare that where Christ is, there is no darkness; where He is, there is wonderful light!

As wonderful as it will be when Christ returns, even Christians want him to wait a little bit until they reach the goals they have set for themselves. Maybe you haven't bought that new car or built that new house. Maybe you haven't seen all your grandchildren graduate from high school.

A friend told me the story of his father, who always had the desire to see all of his grandchildren finish high school. As a matter of fact, it was recently that his dad attended the graduation of his youngest grandson, and felt such pride and satisfaction. He sat and watched the ceremony unfold, and he was so very thankful to be at that place at that time. He wasn't feeling well, so he found a chair behind the bleachers in the gym. He did not want to interfere with the festivities. It was there in that chair that his lifeless body was found, still smiling at the accomplishment of seeing each and every one of his grandchildren graduate. He had reached his goal.

He had asked to live to see his grandchildren finish high school, and he was granted that time here on earth. On the day we were born, we all came with an expiration date. My friend's dad reached that date at the exact time

Peter ONE

he desired. Christ will return at the exact time the Father deems appropriate.

But if you actually talk about the return of The Son of God, many of your closest friends may classify you as a kook. Make no mistake – Jesus is coming back! As believers, we need to be prepared for him in our hearts at all times. We need to encourage one another with these words and actually look forward with anticipation for our King's return.

1:6 In all this you greatly rejoice, though now for a little while you may have had to suffer grief in all kinds of trials.

Suffer? We may have to suffer? Oh man, I was hoping that once I became a Christian, my suffering would be over. I was hoping that all my stupid mistakes would be behind me. How about you? Were you hoping that too? Well, the fact is that we belong to our Father God now. When we accepted Christ as Lord and Savior, we were born again. Our spirits are regenerated as God's own. But we still inhabit this flesh, this earthly body, and we still have our human minds. With our minds, we make choices. God wants us to make good choices – and, of course, many of them are – but some of them are not!

He never saves people from sin and death to become robots! So when Peter says, *"Greatly rejoice,"* he is saying that our faith is found only in the mercy and grace of God. We may fall, but we can get up and keep moving. We may have to "suffer grief" and all kinds of

Peter ONE

trials, but it is for a little while. When we struggle with sin and find ourselves in a trial that shakes us to the core, we must find a way to persevere. Regardless of how we feel or what we think, our failures, our sin, our pain, and our shortcomings, we are here but for a "little while." Even if this struggle lasts years, it is a short time compared to eternity.

Many of the issues we bring about start in the mind, and the battlefield of the mind is a very real place. The mind has taken more lives than all the world wars combined. That is why we are instructed in **Romans 12:2**, *"Do not conform any longer to the pattern of this world, but be transformed by the renewing of your mind."*

Friend, we are to renew our minds in the solid, reliable word of God on a daily basis. Renewing our minds in God's word is for our good. In the word of God we find hope, instruction, and power. So why do so few of us allow the time to take advantage of this renewing? Could it be that we have become so bombarded with technology that we miss the simple truth and deep transforming words that come from reading the Bible? Yes, there is that, and then there is the enemy of us all, busyness. We are much too busy to spend the first part of our day renewing our minds. "I have way too much on my mind to try to read and meditate on the Bible". This is the sad truth of the matter.

The renewing of our minds in the Word of God, allows us to stand in times of trouble. It readies us for life's challenges, and it creates a yearning to praise God for the living hope found in Christ.

Peter ONE

Christ is coming back. So, be encouraged, and continue to grow deep in the things of the Holy Spirit of God. Live as if he could come back today. If he does, let him find us a people of prayer, hope, and praise, as we live only for him. Yes, we will have trials. Jesus said, *"In this world you will have trouble,"* but we are to rejoice, for he has overcome the world!
The grief and the trials are unfortunately a part of this human condition, and our Father allows them in our life. Why?

1:7 These have come so that the proven genuineness of your faith, of greater worth than gold, which perishes even though refined by fire, may result in praise, glory and honor when Jesus Christ is revealed.

Can our faith really be that important? There are many mentions of this attribute in the New Testament. Faith is mentioned 245 times in the New Testament. How we use this word, together with hope and love, is a cornerstone of a Christian's belief system. When Paul states, *"Our faith is of greater value than gold,"* it makes sense. It adds up.

Speaking of adding up, have you seen the price of gold lately? I mean, it is priced by the ounce when we buy or sell it, not the pound. Come to think of it, I have heard the expression "an ounce of faith," but never a pound or gallon or cup of faith. Men have for centuries placed value on gold. It is measured by purity, and that is why Peter speaks of refining by fire in his statement about

Peter ONE

having a genuine faith. Gold can be mixed with other metals and still remain shiny, but to prove and refine the true gold, it must undergo extreme heat. The fire hot enough to melt gold will also melt lesser metals to expose the imperfection of gold filled with other metal and bits of foreign particles.

As the refiner's fire melts the metal, the other metals and particles float to the top, where they are skimmed and removed. This dross is the scum that forms on the surface of melted metal. It is waste or foreign matter that must be removed to produce pure gold.

Your faith is more precious than the purest gold, so why wouldn't you want to be refined? Because it's a painful process! We think that our faith will somehow grow on its own, just in the days, weeks, months, or years that go by. No – it doesn't get better with age like wine or cheese, unless we focus on growing it.

Peter says the grief and trial are to refine our faith. The heat of going through trouble should produce the "dross" of this life, the scum that is revealed through the process. At that point, we make the choice to remove the scum, or we turn down the heat and cover up the imperfections with impure gold. I want to be made pure. How about you? If so, then we have to go through the fire to test the purity and value of our faith.

When we are proved genuine after the fire, we know Christ in us, and the most pure is revealed. We praise and honor Father God as a result. To God goes all the

Peter ONE

glory. We are in this together. Pray for me, that when my refining fire burns bright and hot, the dross of my faith be removed; I will do the same for you. We will be better off as a result of our faith being tested and proven. We will be pure and useful to the Master.

1:8 Though you have not seen him, you love him; and even though you do not see him now, you believe in him and are filled with an inexpressible and glorious joy,

1:9 for you are receiving the end result of your faith, the salvation of your souls.

Peter is writing to "God's elect," other believers who have never seen Jesus in the flesh. They appear to love him and believe in him, and for some reason they are filled with great joy! They have placed their faith in the Savior but have never laid their physical eyes on Jesus. That would be us, too. Yes, Peter is writing to us, too. When we believe in the Lord Jesus and put our faith in him, we say, "Yes, Lord, we will trust and obey."

Think of it in terms of the Lord's army. We enlist – "join up," as it were – and enter basic training. We read the Word of God, we see how wonderful the mercy and grace of God is, and we become grateful to be counted among the believers. The more we are exposed to our Savior, the more we love, respect, and want to serve. We may not have met him in the physical flesh, in person, but we trust, obey, and become good soldiers.

Peter ONE

Of course, we have not seen Christ face to face yet, but our spirits become more one with him as we seek after more of God.

Jesus is the best friend you could ever have. You talk to him, love him, and trust him with your very life. He gives us great gifts, because he loves us. Gifts like life, joy, peace, mercy, grace, love, relationship, and breath. But he doesn't stop there. We get those perfect moments, when we look into the eyes of our three year old son, and he says, "I love you Daddy." Or we hold our five-pound granddaughter, who just couldn't wait to get to this world to see us. Every day is a gift he has given us. Our gift back to him should be what we do with the gifts he gives us. When we live out our faith, our refined faith that is more valuable than gold, it is because he gives us the gift of our next breath.

No, we have not seen him face to face, as Peter had so many times in the three years he was with him. But we love him. Today, as you go about the simple and not so simple tasks of life on earth, let me encourage you to glorify God the Father in all you do. Give him the gift of obedience, the gift of praise, and the gift of a life changed and committed to him.

The Lord's heart will be glad. The angels will rejoice, and your life will find a peace that could not exist without this beautiful, redeemed life. After all, we are living out the salvation of our souls.

Peter ONE

1:10 Concerning this salvation, the prophets, who spoke of the grace that was to come to you, searched intently and with the greatest care...
1:11 ... trying to find out the time and circumstances to which the Spirit of Christ in them was pointing when he predicted the sufferings of the Messiah and the glories that would follow.

The prophets spoke of the grace that was to come to us. God communicated throughout the Old Testament that there would come a time when the Messiah would appear on earth, bring salvation to God's people, and redeem mankind of the certain death that was produced by the fall of man. This death became certain when Adam chose disobedience and unknowingly continued Lucifer's rebellion against God. But Lucifer, the fallen angel we call Satan, became God's enemy. With the fall in the garden, sin entered this new type of being called man.

Created in God's image and given the garden to tend, this man was blessed by the Creator. The fall doesn't make sense in light of this blessing. From the time of the fall, right up to the time of Christ's appearance on the scene, man struggled to live by the Law. Man struggled, because it really was impossible to keep all of it.

Man needed a once-and-for-all sin sacrifice, a perfect lamb of God. The lamb's blood would save all of mankind from sin and hell. Trust me on this point: no

Peter ONE

matter how good a person is on the outside, it is the lamb's blood that saves each and every "good" or "bad" person from a lifetime and beyond of consequences of sin. This perfect blood saves from an eternity of Hell. Yes, the prophets foretold Jesus's coming. They told of the grace that was found in the womb of Mary. They also foretold of a savior who would hang on a tree. The cross at the Place of the Skull, Golgotha, fulfilled the prophecy. He came as a baby and lived holy, and then he died as a common thief to bring us a powerful and uncommon life. When we are found in him, and he in us, this grace the world knows little of becomes rich and real in our lives here on earth.

When Peter talks of the *"glories to follow,"* we get a glimpse into the acts of the early church. Jesus said, *"Greater works you shall do."* What does that mean? We may long for such a time, but let me ask you: have you done any of those recently? Do you know of any greater works? Me neither. Or do we?

When we encourage people to occupy until Jesus comes back, we are not telling people to just wait things out until Jesus comes back. "Just hang in there. This life is but a wisp, and then we are out of here." No, we need to encourage each other with the knowledge of the prophets. Jesus is surely coming back, but when we say to occupy, that is not to encourage people just to take up space on planet Earth. Occupying is being a participant in the glories that are present every day.

Peter ONE

1:12 It was revealed to them that they were not serving themselves but you, when they spoke of the things that have now been told you by those who have preached the gospel to you by the Holy Spirit sent from heaven. Even angels long to look into these things.

What do we do with truth? When it becomes truth revealed, and not just truth to our minds but truth to our hearts, change happens. True change does not take place until the heart is engaged.

Yes, the prophets who spoke and wrote of the birth, death, and resurrection of the Messiah longed to see it come to pass. Some of them, compelled by the Holy Spirit, wrote accounts of these experiences, and we followers of Christ Jesus now have the joy of seeing without actually having been there. That, my friend, is called faith.

Read **Hebrews 11:1** in the King James version:

*"**Now faith is the substance of things hoped for, the evidence of things not seen.**"*

Not seeing, but believing. The world would say, "Seeing is believing." You decide: how deep is your faith?

The quiet joy of knowing him, of loving him because he first loved us, is amazing. When I was a child, I saw pictures of Jesus, but they didn't satisfy my curiosity. There were several, but he looked a bit different in

Peter ONE

some. The most famous in my mind was the one we had hanging in our home. Maybe some of you have seen it. This picture of Jesus had a golden glow – even the robe glowed. In it, Jesus had shoulder length hair and a sweet smile. I really liked that picture. It somehow communicated that no matter the struggles, and there were many in my childhood, everything was going to be well. It was just a picture, yes, but as a child, I loved him because he first loved me.

Then, to find out there is a place for me in Heaven, a reservation! I heard there was a place booked for me and ready for when the time comes, and with childlike faith I believe it. So, we have our reservations, and we know that this Earth is not our true home.

A few years ago, I finally got hold of that. I came to realize the houses, the cars, and the stuff – all wood, hay, stubble – will fade away. As they fade, my place in Heaven becomes brighter and brighter. Even angels greatly desire to understand more about these things!

One of the greatest problems today for men is identify theft. No, not your credit cards or bank account, but your true identity found in Christ. The enemy of your soul would like nothing more than to get you feeling like you're a failure. You are a failure at marriage, or at being a father, or at business, or at relationships, or in finances. You get the picture. Satan hates the idea of you loving and worshipping the one true God, so his aim is to destroy your witness for Christ.

Peter ONE

I had a man tell me the other day that he feels like a phony. He is in ministry, but he struggles with temptation and has not felt productive. Have you ever felt like that? I have. It is not that we won't go through times in which we fail; it's that we don't stay in that failure and accept it as a part of our life!

You were made for a purpose, and if we lose who we are in Christ, guess what? We lose. We live in a fallen world full of ungodliness, and when we become no different than the world and full of the world's ways, we lose much more than we can ever gain. We lose our identity. If we fail to live as Christ followers while we call ourselves Christians, we lose.

When Peter lays it out for us, he reminds us that the Prophets served us by giving us insights into what God has planned for us. Our Father has us living and breathing here today as a part of his bigger story. Right here, right now, if you have chosen to live for Christ. And because of that choice, you have a mission. We are to reach the lost. We are to go and make disciples of all nations. The Great Commission was not just for the saints alive that witnessed Jesus's death and resurrection it is for now, this call is part of our true identity. We can and will be used of God, when we finally and totally surrender to his plan. You ready?

When we are found in Christ alone, we have such a focus on the eternal that the external cannot drag us down to the point where we forget who we are and to whom we belong. Yes, we all fail, but we must get up and move forward. Do me a favor, and lay this book down. Close your eyes, and ask our Father what your next step is. Do not think about all the earthly limitations or your past failures. He knows all things. Just ask him for the next step. Too many of us want the whole picture all at once, or we are unwilling to step at all. Don't worry God's got it all in his hands. He just wants your faith in action, and he wants your obedience. So, just ask what your next step is. Once that is revealed, go for it!

Be Holy

1:13 Therefore, with minds that are alert and fully sober, set your hope on the grace to be brought to you when Jesus Christ is revealed at his coming.
In the NIV translation, this section of 1 Peter has the heading of *"Be Holy."* Growing up, I was exposed to many parts of the U.S. We moved often; my stepdad was a surveyor for the Bureau of Reclamation at the time. At one point, we lived in an area of the country where there were churchgoers. When we saw the women dressed in long dresses, their hair up in buns, and the men's shirts buttoned up to the very top button, they appeared very different from us. At least, they were different on the outside.

Some people referred to them as "Holy Rollers." Was it the way they looked or how they lived that earned them that term? I am not sure, but we are instructed to: *prepare our minds, be self-controlled, and set our hope fully on grace.* These are all inner actions and not outward appearance. Sometimes we get so hung up on

Peter ONE

the way people look, we miss the fact that God is working in their hearts.

I don't particularly care for tattoos, but I have friends who have several. I know one guy who uses his to witness to the lost – the large cross on his left forearm is a conversation starter, and the people he comes in contact with need "Christ-centered conversations." Larry is my biker buddy, and he uses that tattoo as a kingdom tool. Maybe it is really a "tattool". It is not the tattoo; it is his heart to reach people, that counts.

You can put one of those silver fish on the back of your car to make a statement of faith, but when a car cuts you off in traffic, there could be problems! Or cars with bumper stickers that read, "God is my Co-pilot," and, "Give Peace a Chance." Can you picture that? Kind of crazy what traffic and bad drivers can do to us! Holy Road Rage Batman! Here is the point, we need to prepare our minds for action, as in **Romans 12:2:** "Do not conform any longer to the pattern of this world, but be transformed by the renewing of your mind."

This is the action of renewal. The focus is on the inside, to be single-minded. James points out in **James 1:8***:* *"A double-minded man is unstable in all he does."* Are we single-minded, seeking after kingdom opportunities? Are we preparing our minds for action? Are we self-controlled? The answer of course is Yes and No. I would love to just say, "Yes," but the fact is that I fail. I used to hope that being a Christian would mean never sinning, but the reality is that we live in a fallen world that is full of sin. When I stumble, I must rely on forgiveness,

Peter ONE

grace, and mercy of a loving Father, to restore fellowship. My 24/7 is just that, seven days a week. I need the grace of Christ 365 days a year, and 366 during a leap year.

As a sinner saved by grace, I have been brought into the Family of God. My goal is to walk in righteousness every day of my life, knowing I can do something every day (365) of my life for advancing the Kingdom. We may not be able to live up to 24/7, but we can definitely do something each day for his glory, setting our hope fully on the grace given to us!

1:14 As obedient children, do not conform to the evil desires you had when you lived in ignorance.
1:15 But just as he who called you is holy, so be holy in all you do;

1:16 for it is written: "Be holy, because I am holy."

So Peter reminds us to live as we are – made whole in Christ. He reminds us to be holy. We are not perfect, but due to God's grace and mercy that was poured out on us through his Son Jesus, we don't have to "act" Holy. We are made his righteous people

I'm sure you have seen people who try to act Holy, but who only come across as judgmental or pious. Thank God that we do not have to "act" anything. We just need to "be" followers of Christ. We need to be obedient,

Peter ONE

walking in truth and not stumbling in ignorance as we did before we came to Christ. I don't know about you, but before I was saved I was a "nice guy." However, I still only lived for whatever made me happy. My decisions were all about me. My actions were to make me look good. My deceptive nature ruled the day.

I was ignorant of the things of God. I knew of Jesus; I just did not know Him. On that November day decades ago, everything changed! Evil desires? Yes, they were driven out. Selfish ambitions? They sometimes try to jump up, but that is when I must cover my multitude of sins with the blood of Christ.

I spoke at a men's event recently, and I challenged them to sound the battle cry in their life. Realizing we are at war here on planet Earth, the question is, "Are you a POW, or are you Free?" We must not walk in ignorance, disobedient to the commander. We must stand together, putting on the whole armor of God. Remember that he who has called us is Holy. We are made whole in Christ so that we may be Holy in all we do. We are Holy, because he is Holy.

1:17 Since you call on a Father who judges each person's work impartially, live out your time as foreigners here in reverent fear.

I love this verse. Peter lets us know. Look, God is no respecter of people, and he judges each of us impartially. Wow! Our Father does not play favorites. Don't you wish everyone were like that? But then he

Peter ONE

says to live in reverent fear. Ok, I get the reverence part, but to live in fear? We must remember that we are not dealing with another man who can be fooled with our outward emotions, but that we are dealing with a Father who knows us better than we know ourselves. He knows us from the inside out.

In a sense, Peter is saying to be honest with God, to honor him with your truthful heart, for he is the one who set you free. His Son paid the price for you and I. His blood flowed on Calvary and is flowing still to redeem all who would say, "Yes!" So, respect the Father as creator and redeemer, and live a life in the light of salvation. It is sad and disturbing to me to see a person who was brought out of a life of sin by the work of Jesus Christ treat their salvation with little regard. Or worse, people sometimes turn their backs on our Savior, and they return to a life of destruction.
My friend, may it never be that we take our salvation for granted or return to our old life. We are not POW's; WE ARE FREE. And may every day be a loving, rejoicing tribute to the one who set us free.

Of course, when Peter says to live as strangers here, he means this planet. Heaven is our home. It is where we are going, and it is where our true family resides.

When we get so comfortable with the enemy territory we find ourselves in, we lose focus on what is to come. We read in Exodus how God's people left Egypt. After they were held captive and treated ruthlessly by the Egyptians day after day for 430 years, they left Egypt led by Moses. They crossed the Red Sea with dry feet!

Peter ONE

They drank bitter water that was made sweet, they had quail and manna, and they still grumbled.

Really? Does it sound familiar? Oh, and then they received water from a rock. All of this happened after they were set free from their captors, the Egyptians. It sounds like they should and possibly could stop the grumbling, complaining, and doubting. After all, these are people – you know, men and women who have seen the miracles of God. But no...

So, my question is: Have we not been delivered? Have we not been taken out of the enemy camp, been given food and drink, and set free? Yes! We should operate with a grateful heart and with thanksgiving, but do we?

Back to the Israelites: what did they do? Did they cry out to glorify God? No, they complained and took matters into their own hands. They eventually made a golden calf to worship. You may think that they especially were a bunch of ungrateful people, but when you hold your faith up to God's light, do you see any cracks? I know I do, but he is still working on me. So, I live my life as a stranger here on earth, in reverent fear.

1:18 For you know that it was not with perishable things such as silver or gold that you were redeemed from the empty way of life handed down to you from your ancestors,

1:19 but with the precious blood of Christ, a lamb without blemish or defect.

Peter ONE

Oh, what a price was paid for our redemption. Peter reminds us that even silver and gold pass away, are perishable, and were not valuable enough to purchase our freedom. The valuable metals of the day were not enough – only the precious blood of Christ. The perfect one was enough. When Peter writes, *"When you redeemed from the empty way of life handed down to you from your forefathers,"* what comes to mind? For me, this statement sums up my life.

Before I knew Christ as Lord and Savior, my life was empty, desperate, and lonely. Sure, I had some family and friends, but deep in my heart I felt like damaged goods. My forefathers literally were my four fathers, including my stepfathers. My biological father left when I was six weeks old, and my mom was stuck with three kids to raise. We knew beyond a shadow of doubt that she loved each and every one of us and did her best.

She ended up in another marriage that lasted a few years. I had two older siblings and three younger, three sisters and two brothers – six kids from four different fathers. I don't remember having any spiritual guidance from any of my four fathers, so when Peter writes of an empty way of life, I relate. As an adult, I continued to try to fill that emptiness with things of this world, but I still felt like damaged goods.

Not long ago, I had a conversation with Jim Daly, the President of Focus on the Family. In that conversation, he made a statement that resonated with me. He said *"Mel, men who have been through what we have been through are connected. They are the fraternity*

Peter ONE

fatherless." I took what he was saying to mean, that no matter what our childhood looked like – no matter how small and insignificant we appear in our own eyes; there is a loving father who thinks so highly of us that he was willing to send his Son to die a horrible death on a cross to save us from a horrible eternity in Hell.

Oh, the peace and freedom I felt when I realized that! What about you? Do you know the greatest Father of all time? Do you know Father God, who loves you just like you are? He can take you, make you, and fill you to overflowing with his peace and love, and he can take the empty life of our forefathers and make it something beautiful for him.

My friend, that is more valuable than silver and gold. To know this Dad will not leave us and will never desert us, but that he always wants the very best for us. All we need to do is trust him, and realize he gives us our next breath. That breath is life giving so we may bring glory to our Father.

The blood of God's perfect lamb redeems you and I. The sacrifice of the Holy Lamb, without blemish or defect, has bought us. His blood was absolutely more than enough. Take a look at this old writing from Edward Mote:

Peter ONE

The Solid Rock

**His oath, His covenant, His Blood,
Support me in the whelming flood.
When all around my soul gives way,
He then is all my hope and stay.
On Christ the solid rock I stand,
All other ground is sinking sand.**
                    -Edward Mote (1797-1874)

Written centuries ago, these words stand true today, *"On Christ the solid rock I stand, all other ground is sinking sand, all other ground is sinking sand."*

Back to First Peter;

1:20 He was chosen before the creation of the world, but was revealed in these last times for your sake.

1:21 Through him you believe in God, who raised him from the dead and glorified him, and so your faith and hope are in God.

Jesus is, was, and will always be. He was revealed as a man, at God's chosen time, as part of the Holy Trinity: God the Father, God the Son, and God the Holy Spirit. It was the Son who was sent to Earth and born of a virgin. He grew up as the son of an earthly father and mother, and he saw all of the human condition. That God came to shed his own blood for you and I proves

Peter ONE

he loves us. He loved us before our first breath, and he will love us long after we take our last breath, here on earth.

Peter says Christ was *"revealed in these last times for your sake."* What do you think and how do you feel about Christ Jesus? Have you had a full revelation of his great love? Has it deeply changed every aspect of your life? He is always willing to do that, to change us from the inside out. Please, please, please: if you have not let him have total access to your heart and mind, now is the time.

What was the order in which you believed? Did you believe in God and then Jesus? Or was it accepting the beautiful life that Christ offered, and then God came with the deal? It really does not matter. The truth is that you can't have one without the other. There are world religions that know of God but do not recognize Jesus as the Son of God. What do we do with that? Well, the truth is as Jesus says. Jesus said in **John 14:6-7**, *"I am the way and the truth and the life. No one comes to the Father except through me. If you really know me, you will know my Father as well."* From now on you do know him and have seen him. So, through Christ our faith and hope are placed in a mighty God. We believe in what we have not seen, because the evidence is everywhere.

Someone once said, "The evidence of God's presence far outweighs the proof of his absence." The evidence is everywhere, and our personal relationship with Jesus gives us access to the Glory of God. The power of the

Peter ONE

Holy Spirit and the mercy and grace of a loving Savior are available – wow! Can you feel in your heart the love that saved us?

1:22 Now that you have purified yourselves by obeying the truth so that you have sincere love for each other, love one another deeply, from the heart

Have you ever loved someone deeply from the heart? In our world, love is so misunderstood. The songs we hear, the movies we watch – is that really what love is? To quote Tina Turner: *"What's love got to do with it?"* Actually, true love has everything to do with it!

Here is the issue. When pop culture uses love in songs and movies, many times we miss the true picture. Here are a couple of lines from Turner's Grammy award-winning song from 1984: *"What's love got to do, got to do with it. What's love but a second hand emotion. What's love got to do, got to do with it, who needs a heart, when a heart can be broken."*

(Writer(s): Terry Britten, Joe Bihari, Riley B. King
Copyright: Unviversal Music- Careers, WB Music Corp.)

Did you see that? "Who needs a heart, when a heart can be broken." I know, it's just a lyric from a song, but have you ever met someone who lives life with that philosophy? It is a sad commentary on the state of modern man.

In 1850, Alfred Lord Tennyson wrote a poem called "In Memorian:27." In it, we read a famous quote: *"Tis better to have loved and lost than never to have loved at all."* I

Peter ONE

guess I come down on the side of risking love and my heart. God has given us love, and he has shown us true love. He loves the whole world.

Read this familiar scripture: ***"For God so loved the world that he gave his one and only son, that whoever believes in him should not perish but have eternal life" (John 3:16).***

Now that's love, when you make a way of escape for all of mankind. But unfortunately not all will receive the wonderful gift and accept Christ as the redeemer, let alone the Lord. God the Father knows that. But he does not want anyone to perish to a life of torment in the chambers of Hell.

Yes, God loves you. Yes, he gave his Son for you. Yes, he is waiting. So, why say, "No," to all he has done? Why not accept this love that is deeper than any human love? This is what Peter is referring to. We are purified by truth, remember? The truth shall set you free (John 8:32), and when we are free in truth we are purified. We obey, and we actually have the capacity to love deeply. Most likely our love is not deep, abiding love. It may be that we need to ask the burning questions proposed by another song. The Brothers Gibb, or The BeeGee's, as they were known. In one of their songs, they ask the question, *"How deep is your love?"* Here is the chorus: *"How deep is your love? I really need to learn cause we're living in a world of fools, breaking us down when they all should let us be, we belong to you and me."*
(How Deep is Your Love lyrics, Warner Chappell Music, Inc. Universal Music Publishing Group.)

The Other Guy who Walked on Water!

Peter ONE

Peter says truth gives us sincere love for our brothers. We can love deeply from the heart, and it makes more sense than an old love song or one of those romantic comedy films that keeps us hopeful that love will find us one day. News flash – love has found you. His name is Jesus, and he loves you and wants the very, very best for you. Trust him.

1:23 For you have been born again, not of perishable seed, but of imperishable, through the living and enduring word of God.

1:24 For, "All people are like grass, and all their glory is like the flowers of the field; the grass withers and the flowers fall,

1:25 but the word of the Lord endures forever. And this is the word that was preached to you.

I have been known to be fairly direct, and I think Peter is laying out a direct idea here, speaking to all who have a heart to hear. We have been born again through imperishable seed in Jesus Christ, God's loving and enduring word. Let me ask you a direct question, the most important direct question you could ever be asked:

Do you know that Jesus has saved you, that you belong to him, that He lives in your heart, and that you are free in Christ? Now, that direct question deserves a direct answer. Is it, "Yes," or is it, "No?"

Peter ONE

Notice that I never asked, "Do you know Jesus?" That's like asking if you know a Mustang. You know, the car made by Ford. Well, you may say you do. But if you don't own a Mustang, sit on those nice leather seats, change the oil, fill the gas tank, or a hundred other things that go into owning a Mustang, do you really know a Mustang? No. You might know of Jesus, but do you know him as your Lord? That is a direct question. What is your direct answer?

Peter makes a statement that should create a sense of urgency. *"All men are like grass, and all their glory is like the flowers of the field."* Ok, flowers look better than grass, but the idea here is that both will eventually wither and fall away. Men, you and I will die, and when we do, our glory dies with us. But God's glory continues forever!

We are here on planet Earth for just a short time. Some of us may have more days than others, but we all come with an expiration date. Peter's point is to teach this. Make eternal decisions while you are in this temporary place. Yes, this kingdom of Earth is temporary, and the Kingdom of God is forever. Our hope of glory is placed in Christ Jesus, who will forever be. When we follow him here on Earth and we pass away, our blade of grass dies and withers, and our flower dries up. He still is – we will continue to worship him and all his glory for eternity.

We are given these short years on Earth to make that decision. To answer the most important question you will ever answer: Is Christ Jesus your Lord and Savior?

Peter ONE

If yes, then let's be about our Father's business. Let's live in the peace and joy that the world does not know. Let them see that there is something different, and make them curious to know. Walk as a child of God for as long as you are here. Keep your grass green and your flowers beautiful for Christ until you are called to your one true home in glory!

2:1 Therefore, rid yourselves of all malice and all deceit, hypocrisy, envy, and slander of every kind.

Peter just laid out the glory of our God: the integrity and power found in reading and trusting the Word of God. Now he tells us that, since we have been exposed to the word, we are to receive it as a child of God.

We are to get rid of all malice, deceit, hypocrisy, envy, and slander. If these are out of our lives, what does that look like? What replaces them? I am reminded of the life of Jesus. His heart was pure. In him, there was no deceit, hypocrisy, envy, or slander.

We are created in the image of our God. Peter lists these negative attributes and says to get rid of them. He is saying to purge the sin from our lives. He wants us to start acting like a loved and valued child of God. When we continue to let these sins abide in us, we continue to live the way of the old man, or maybe the way we do not want to, but do anyway, even though Christ died for our sins, and was resurrected in power for our lives.

Peter ONE

Listen, my friend. He died for us, and the least we can do is to live for him. When we read the eternal Word of God and really seek what he is saying to us, it is amazing how our lives can change. But we must read with that intent. I remember thinking years ago that the stories in the Bible were great, even though I couldn't pronounce some of the names. I read and re-read the One Year Bible. I had a goal to read the complete Word of God from front to back! I did that, but now that I am older and much wiser (I am smiling), I realize that God's Word is to be read with our hearts as well as with our minds. As Paul says, when we rid ourselves of the daily nonsense, we can come to the Word like a babe that desires its mother's milk. We get hungry for the truth.

2:2 Like newborn babies, crave pure spiritual milk, so that by it you may grow up in your salvation,

2:3 now that you have tasted that the Lord is good.

The Lord is good. The Lord is God. God is good. God is love. No matter how you speak the truth, it sounds sweet. Doesn't it?

Peter is challenging us to grow up in our salvation. He challenges us to understand that, yes, we come as children to the Lord, and, yes, we are dependent on him for everything, but that we are to grow in our salvation.

Most people think that growing up is becoming more independent, but the fact is that when we grow in our Salvation, we become more and more dependent on our

Peter ONE

loving Father. In Corinthians 13:11, we read: *"When I was a child, I talked like a child, I thought like a child, I reasoned like a child. When I become a man, I put the ways of childhood behind me."*

People talk about the second childhood of life, meaning our elderly population. In an affectionate way, we do see some of the same attributes of a child in people reaching the ends of their journey. But we must remember that we are on this journey, and a journey of a thousand miles starts with just the first step.

Our faith walk is just that: a walk, which implies that there is movement. Steps must be taken, and when those steps are taken, things happen.

Your faith and my faith was intended to grow. When we are in motion due to the steps we are taking, the surroundings change. Friends who are not growing are left behind, and the bad choices and stupid decisions get farther and farther away. As we grow in this Salvation, we put away the childish things of the past.

We gain strength with each step of this journey, provided that we are on the right path. We grow up; facing each obstacle and every hurdle with knowledge we obtain from the reading of God's Word. The Word is our nourishment for the journey.

Let me ask you: are you growing? Has your faith become stagnate? Are you no further down the path than you were five years ago? It is time to grow, to take your salvation seriously, and to put away childish distractions. It is time to quit acting like you did as a kid. Grow up, and take your place among the adults at the table. Let me explain.

Peter ONE

When I was a kid, every holiday that we got together as a family, there were so many people that the children had a couple "special" tables of their own. They were card tables set within a safe distance from the big table, where my Mom and all the adults sat.

We had little chairs, little dishes, and little spoons and forks. We had our food cut up for us, and someone had already put the green beans on our plate! We had it made for a time. I remember thinking,

"Someday, I will get to sit at the big table." And I did.

I remember sitting up straight, holding my fork correctly and chewing my food with my mouth closed.

My mom said that if we "smacked" (chewed with our mouth open) at the table, we would get smacked (a love pat or stronger somewhere on the anatomy where it made a point). Of course that was in a day when families ate together at the table, had conversation, and you could actually hear if someone was chewing with their mouth open. We called it smacking, and in a day when manners actually meant something it was important not to do it.

I realized sitting at the big table, it was the same food, but with a larger table, larger chairs, and larger dishes. I became a smaller person at the big table, instead of being a bigger person at the smaller table. Are you getting this picture?

Many people today want to stay at the kids' table. I know 30-year-old guys who play more video games than most 12-year-olds, for example. Grown "boys" who want to sit at the kids' table don't look very appealing. We need to

Peter ONE

grow up, spiritually speaking, and take our places at the big table.

Stop making excuses about your past, or about the bad things that are holding you back. Peter says to grow up in your Salvation, now that you have tasted and know that the Lord is good.

The Living Stone and a Chosen People

2:4 As you come to him, the living Stone—rejected by humans but chosen by God and precious to him—

2:5 you also, like living stones, are being built into a spiritual house to be a holy priesthood, offering spiritual sacrifices acceptable to God through Jesus Christ.

A living stone, chosen by God and rejected by men. We are like living stones that are being built into a spiritual house. When Peter paints this picture, we see the example that the early church would have recognized. God is building a spiritual temple, a house of faith, using living stones (us) that are made alive in Christ. Christ is the precious foundation of this building project.

This spiritual house is built on Christ alone, the Hope of Glory. The temple of old was a house for God's glory, but Christ's work upon the cross not only saved mankind, but it also restored our access to God's glory. In Matthew 27:51, we read, *"At that moment the curtain of the temple was torn in two from top to bottom"*

Peter ONE

The moment when God watched his son die for all men, God restored access to himself, and the curtain of the temple was torn. We read this and see there was an earthquake, and maybe we assume this curtain was torn because of that. But, upon further investigation, we see that this "curtain" was not made of lace, like the curtains at Grandma's house. No, this was more like a huge rug. It was 60 feet long, 30 feet wide, and 4 inches thick! It took 300 priests just to handle this veil. The temple curtain was torn from top to bottom by God, signifying that there are no more barriers between God and man. Jesus restored our relationship with God, because of love.

Peter says the temple was built with cornerstones. In Solomon's temple, the chief cornerstone is said to have measured a mere 3 feet and 8 inches high by 14 feet long. But what is more important is that it rested on solid rock. That was a temple built by the hands of men. You and I are temples built by the hands of God.

We are living stones, and our spiritual houses are built on the ultimate living stone, Jesus Christ. But Peter goes on: *"to be built into a spiritual house, a Holy priesthood to offer up spiritual sacrifices acceptable to God through Jesus Christ."*

A Holy priesthood? You and I are priests? Yes, in the sense that we no longer require a trip to the temple with our doves, goats, calves, or lambs for a sin offering. The once-and-for-all sin offering was given at Calvary. Jesus is our high priest, and he has given us access into the Holy of Holies. He has called us to be the priest of our homes.

Peter ONE

"Priest" is mentioned 161 times in the New Testament, and many of those times it is associated with teachers of the law or teachers of the scriptures. Today, we are to be the teachers, the leaders, and the priests, ready to give ourselves to our God for service. Remember, we can only serve as priests in Christ Jesus. On our own, we have no authority.

We are living stones set on the Rock of Ages. We are priests in our homes, a people of God that brings spiritual sacrifices that are acceptable to God through Christ alone. In Revelation 1:5-6, we read, *"To him who loves us and has freed us from our sins by his blood, and has made us to be a kingdom and priests to serve his God and Father – to him be glory and power forever and ever! Amen."*

God has always provided. When we read of Adam and Eve, we see that a wonderful garden was provided. Noah and his family were provided a means of escape. Abraham was provided a ram in the thicket, in order to sacrifice it instead of having to sacrifice his son.

All through the Word, we read of God's provision. All through the ages God has provided for his people. Today is no exception. What has he provided for you? Think about it: a home, a car, a bank account. Yes, but what about your family, or your kids? Our Father cares so much about us that he has provided a way of escape. We no longer have to walk in sin, but are set free. We are living and breathing because of God's grace.

We can know that goodness and mercy will follow us all the days of our lives, and we can know we are the temple of the Holy Spirit.

Peter ONE

Are our sacrifices are acceptable to God? We could never offer or add anything to the ultimate sacrifice of Jesus Christ. But when we are given a new life in him, what is our gift back to him? It is a life lived in this freedom. We give back to God the only thing we have of value: our redeemed life lived in Christ. He makes us alive, and he alone is our righteousness. Christ alone is our Hope of Glory.

We once were dead, but now we are made alive in Christ. We were dead rocks, but now we are live stones, living only because of his love for us. Now, our Holy and acceptable sacrifice brings glory to God. Make sense? I hope so. That is what Peter is wanting us to realize. Our lives are a spiritual sacrifice to God through Jesus Christ.

We no longer are "dead" rocks, but "living" stones when we move and have our being in Christ Jesus.

2:6 For in Scripture it says:

"See, I lay a stone in Zion,
 a chosen and precious cornerstone,
and the one who trusts in him
 will never be put to shame."

Comparing the Temple of old that was built by human hands to the Temple of the Holy Spirit built by God's hands, we see why Peter included this passage from Isaiah 28:16. We are a living Temple, made out of living parts, with Christ as our chief cornerstone. Built on that foundation, we are part of this great building project.

Peter ONE

We become living stones in the work of God through Christ. We become dwelling places for God's Spirit, and when we do we have a blessed assurance that, when we trust in him, we will not be put to shame.

Picture this. You are the Temple of God's Holy Spirit in Christ. You are strong, because the cornerstone is strong and supports you. You also know that attacks against this Temple will come. They will not prevail, but our enemy is like the urban gang that equips itself with cans of spray paint. They come out in the darkness and try their best to deface God's property, this Temple. You are sprayed with graffiti: words like "Fear," "Shame," "Doubt," and "Confusion."

These words do not change the structure. This Temple rests on the cornerstone, so it's still strong. These attacks do not change the living stones (us). They are ugly, and they are designed to get us off our task of advancing the Kingdom of God. The attack is nothing more than words or discouragement. Well, guess what? These attacks fail.

When we pray to our Father it's as if he sends his cleaning crew. He uses the cleansing agents of love, forgiveness, power, mercy, and grace, and the squad removes the sprayed on words. This living Temple of God is renewed, cleansed, and stands firm as an example of the strength of our Loving God operating through us.

Peter ONE

The sprayed-on paint will not have the victory. We can trust in Him, and the shame that would try to be painted on us is null and void. We are living stones built on a living chief cornerstone, Jesus Christ. We must walk in the victory won by Christ and not succumb to the exterior attack from our enemy. As believers, we should never let shame dictate our actions, other than the action of repentance.

Peter continues on and lays out the truth regarding this capstone, of the continual building project of God, his son Jesus is the Stone

2:7 Now to you who believe, this stone is precious. But to those who do not believe,

**"The stone the builders rejected
has become the cornerstone,"**

2:8 and, "A stone that causes people to stumble and a rock that makes them fall."

They stumble because they disobey the message—which is also what they were destined for.

Jesus has been a stumbling block for man since the beginning. People who want their way and think they have it all figured out struggle with the idea of needing a Savior.

Peter ONE

The Jewish leaders missed it. They could not accept that this sort of a man – a carpenter – could be the Messiah. How could a person of such low status be the one? They were expecting a worldly Kingdom, but God offered them a spiritual Kingdom. They wanted the Messiah to come and overthrow the political and social leaders of the day.

God chose to overthrow the dark hearts of men, to change the world by changing the hearts of men. God could have, with one word, overthrown any and all nations and governments, but he did not. No. Instead, he gave his Son as a sacrifice for all men of all times, that whoever believes in him would have eternal life. That has caused men to stumble.

This eternal life found in God's own Son can be the foundation of a beautiful life lived to the fullest. Or, rejected, it can be the rock that crushes all sin and disobedience. We have a choice. We either accept Christ and build on that cornerstone, or we reject Christ and stumble through life wondering why we feel the way we do, wondering why it seems like sinking sand is beneath our feet.

If you have any doubt about where you stand, let's settle that right now. Romans 10:9-10 reads, *"If you declare with your mouth, 'Jesus is Lord,' and believe in your heart that God raised him from the dead, you will be saved. For it is with your heart that you believe and are justified, and it is with your mouth that you profess your faith and are saved."*

Peter ONE

Then, in verse 13, *"For, 'Everyone who calls on the name of the Lord will be saved.'"*

Everyone? Are you a part of everyone? Am I a part of everyone? Yes, we are. So, here is a very simple prayer. If you pray it, things can be different from this day forward! Believe in your heart, and confess with your mouth:

"Father God, I come to you as a sinner. I need your forgiveness, your love, and your mercy. I am tired of trying to do it on my own. Please, forgive me for my sin. I want your very best for my life, and I believe that your Son Jesus died on the cross for all my sins. I believe he was raised from the dead to give me life. I call on the name of Jesus. I accept him as my Lord and Savior. I repent, and I know that you are my God. Be my Savior and my friend. I want to be your friend forever. I make this declaration freely, and I know Jesus is my Lord. It is in his name that I pray. Thank you Father. I am yours, and you are mine. Amen."

There, it is settled! We have given our lives to Christ Jesus. Our future is secure, and we will be with the Lord God throughout eternity. By the way, eternity is for all time, including this life right now. We don't have to wait until the next life to enjoy his presence. We can experience some of Heaven right here on planet Earth, here and now! You need to be baptized now, and walk in your new faith, get with other believers that will encourage you and help you grow God's way.

Peter ONE

2:9 But you are a chosen people, a royal priesthood, a holy nation, God's special possession, that you may declare the praises of him who called you out of darkness into his wonderful light.

Have you ever been in a place where it was so dark that you couldn't see your hand in front of your face? I am talking about a literal place, not a spiritual one.

When my boys were younger, we went to explore a cave. The entrance was just a small opening, and we had to squeeze through. Once we were in, the path led to a large room with an underground pool of water. With flashlights off, we experienced one of the darkest places I have ever been. You could not see anything.

We saw nothing but total darkness. But our ears did not stop working – we all commented on the darkness and then made our way back to the mouth of the cave. Our eyes had to adjust to the wonderful light, but we were glad to see again!

Peter is using this example. He says that you and I are a chosen people. We have chosen God, and he has called us out of darkness into his wonderful light. This happens when we are born again, when we become new people in Christ. We are chosen, and we are made royal priests. We are brought into the family of God, which is a Holy Nation. Then, he goes on and calls us and makes us a people belonging to God, wow. We are

Peter ONE

his people brought into the family through and by God's son, Jesus Christ.

Trust me, my friend; this relationship with the creator of the universe is such a grace-filled mercy connection that it is better than coming out of that dark cave in the natural. It is leaving the darkness and sin of this world for the wonderful light of God. So, rejoice with me! He has called us out!

2:10 Once you were not a people, but now you are the people of God; once you had not received mercy, but now you have received mercy.

What do you mean? We were not a people? We are persons, right? Peter is referring to the Gentiles, who were scattered individuals with no identity in God.

They were created by God, of course, but they were not recognized as a people group. They were simply Gentile, which is a word used to describe non-Jewish people.

Peter is saying that you were once just scattered individuals, but that now you have been gathered as one family. That family is the People of God. He also tells us that there once was no mercy received, but that now we have received God's grace and mercy. God loves us, and he wants us to show a dark and dying world how great his mercy and love are.

Peter ONE

We once were not a people, but now we are his people. Because of his great love, we are to take this truth to other scattered people, people who, also, can become a part of his family!

2:11 Dear friends, I urge you, as foreigners and exiles, to abstain from sinful desires, which wage war against your soul.

Once again, we read of war. This battle between good and evil has raged since the beginning of time. Because we are now people of God walking in the light, the enemy would love nothing more than to destroy our peace, ruin our witness for God, and leave us once again in the darkness. But Peter reminds us that we are friends of God. We are his children. He is our Father, and, as such, we are aliens and strangers in this world.

Heaven is our true home. Our spirits came from Father God, and they will return there one day. We now are here on planet Earth, and, in this world, there are so many avenues available in order to express our sinful desires. This is war – the war between your flesh and your spirit. The war is between the kingdom of darkness and the Kingdom of God's wonderful light.

This war is every bit as real as the wars we read of in our history books or see on cable news today! But we fight this war on our knees. We overcome sin through the blood of the lamb – Jesus.

Peter ONE

Yes, he is the Lamb of God who takes away the sins of the world, but he is also a warrior who leads God's mighty army. Yes, we can win this war, by "abstaining from sinful desires." It is easy to say, "Just keep your distance from sin while you are in the world." But you and I do not live on an island alone, so we will be faced with the temptation of sin.

I have learned to prepare for battle. You don't take it lightly. We must be equipped and ready for the fight. Let me give you a few suggestions, in no particular order.

TRUST – Trust your commander, Christ Jesus.
OBEY – Walk daily in obedience, following orders.
READ – Stay in the Bible, and sharpen your sword.
STUDY – Memorize at least one scripture per month.
PRAY – Pray as if your family is at stake.
FELLOWSHIP – Get around other believers (warriors).
EQUIP – Attend conferences, and gain resources.
PRAISE – Lift your hearts up to God. Let him fill you to overflowing, and give a victory shout to God!

The key is to drive out all fear and doubt and to replace it with faith and belief.

Picture this. There is a glass of muddy water sitting on a counter. You can look at it and say, "Well, I guess that's not going to quench my thirst," or you can start pouring water into the glass. The more water you pour in, the more mud is flushed out. Eventually, all the muddy water is replaced with clean, clear water

Peter ONE

Our lives are like that. The more things of God we can pour in, the more the old sin-filled parts of us are driven out, replaced by the sweet spirit of the living God.

That, my friend, is how we abstain from sin. Be filled so much with God and his perfect love that drives out sin. The battle is fought and won in the minds and hearts of men, men filled and equipped to battle. CS Lewis refers to it as "Enemy Occupied Territory."

2:12 Live such good lives among the pagans that, though they accuse you of doing wrong, they may see your good deeds and glorify God on the day he visits us.

What? We are expecting a visit from God? Oh, my friend, he is always with us. How many of us scramble around when we get a call, card, text or letter from a family member informing us they are planning a visit. Even your mother-in-law can produce unexplainable actions. We finish projects that have been put off for months, we clean, we plan, and we do our best to make sure everything is as good as it gets.

Years ago, we received word that my in-laws were coming for a visit, and, of course, I was in the middle of a building project. Seriously, I was right in the middle of a remodel. Not to be diminished in the eyes of my mother-in-law, I accomplished building a stone wall, hearth, and fireplace in weeks instead of months. I stayed up late for a week to get it done, and the day before their arrival I put the last stone in place and

Peter ONE

cleaned up the mess. The mortar was still wet when I proudly gave them the grand tour of our old farmhouse, complete with a very new, stone wall!

So how much more should we be prepared for a visit from the Lord? Well, Peter refers to a visit from God. There are several ideas regarding "visitation." Some believe this is the time when God will come to bring judgment on the Jews, or the time when Christians will be called to suffer for Christ. Some believe it will be a time of blessing instead of judgment.

It seems that this visit will be more of a move of the Spirit of God, or of the hearts of men for God's glory. He says to "live such good lives" that even the non-believing people who come into contact with you will see something different. He urges us to live such that our lives would be revealed as upright and honest, true, and full of grace and mercy. Oh, that they may be persuaded by the lives we live to also love and worship Him on the day of God's visit!

He says, *"Behold, here I am! I stand at the door and knock. If anyone hears my voice and opens the door, I will come in and eat with that person, and they with me"* (Revelation 3:20).

So, even when you have been accused of wrongdoing, or made fun of for believing in God, be strong, stand firm, and keep on keeping on. This may very well be your part in the great commission.

Peter ONE

If non-believers see your life lived for Christ, they may want a life like yours. They may desire the kind of peace, joy, and blessed assurance you have. Then, on the Day of God's Visitation, they may turn their lives over to God!

Do you remember your Day of Visitation, when the knock came at the door of your heart? Do you remember when you knew that things had to change, when you opened the door and Christ came in to wrap his loving arms around you? His love and grace, which we do not deserve, lead us to live good lives. It is not we who are good, but it is the God who dwells within us.

Let's encourage each other with these words. Let's live out loud for our Lord, and let the world know that when we enter a room, it's not just us who enters in.

Our loving Father God, who has given us a way of escape from sin and death, enters also. Let the world be put on notice: we belong to the God of the Universe. Therefore, walk in the confidence of the Lord God.

2:13 Submit yourselves for the Lord's sake to every human authority: whether to the emperor, as the supreme authority,

2:14 or to governors, who are sent by him to punish those who do wrong and to commend those who do right.

Peter ONE

Where do you stand on Christianity in politics? I will say, right up front, that I am for it. I will submit to the history, the true history, of our church and to the founding and history of America. We are to submit ourselves, for the Lord's sake, to those in authority, to every law and authority that is not contrary to the Law of God.

I must admit that "submission" has become almost a bad word in our free country, in our country founded on the Constitution and the Bill of Rights. At our start, we were a people who stood up and made a Declaration of Independence from the tyranny of a king. The King of England was the ruler, but through much prayer, worry, and bravery, America was born. We are an independent people who need to be totally dependent on God.

When Peter writes to "*submit yourself,*" we need to understand the context of Roman rule. He had seen first-hand the total disregard for people from the Roman government. When rulers wanted to exercise their authority, they collected more taxes than some could pay. They kept the population in submission through military strength. They were the authority instituted among men, the same authority that crucified our Jesus. But Peter says we need to submit ourselves! We see some of this same power madness happening today.

Politicians who are to serve the public have been transformed into thinking that Government is the answer to all problems. Washington, D.C., has become the new Rome, where power and authority go to the heads of our

Peter ONE

elected public officials, and the belief held by many is that the people work for the Government!

That is such a far cry from where we started as a nation, "for the people, by the people." The founders knew that the hearts of men could be turned away from God. Men were to represent the people for a short time and then return to productive work. We have seen life-long politicians continue with the power grab; this is not what representation means.

So, how do we submit to authority like that and still maintain our Christian views? Practical ideas have been introduced by great men like George Washington, who said, "It is impossible to rightly govern a nation without God and the Bible." Thomas Jefferson said, "When the people fear the government, there is tyranny. When the government fears the people, there is liberty."

We submit to authority, and we follow the law, but we also answer to a higher authority. When a law is in direct conflict with God's law, we must follow our Lord. As I write this, I am reminded of the U.S. law that gives the right of a born, breathing, and functioning human to take life away from another human being before their first breath! In 1973, Roe v. Wade opened the floodgates for a nation to start killing their unborn citizens. As history records our deeds, so it is repeated.

Ever heard of Moleck (see Leviticus 20:1-5)? Read it, and weep. Here is an example of children being sacrificed. Moleck was a huge bronze statue with the

Peter ONE

head of a bull. Inside, a fire burned, and children were placed in the hands of the statue. Then, the arms raised to the mouth as if Moleck were eating! The children fell into the fire and were consumed, while the people who were gathered before Moleck danced and played flutes and tambourines in an attempt to drown out the screams of the victims: (www.pantheon.org/articals/m/moloch.html).

We say, "How horrible, we would never do that!" No, we would rather sacrifice our children before we have to drown out their screams. My heart cries out for these little ones who will never get a chance to live, who will never have life outside the womb. I am not talking about individuals; I am talking about a nation and a world that says this law is okay.

The general estimate is that over 56 million babies have been taken since Roe v. Wade. Fifty-six million human lives. Fifty-six million productive people and taxpayers. Fifty-six million sweet, innocent babies, and we drown out the screams by saying it is the law, that we can't do anything about it!

2:15 For it is God's will that by doing good you should silence the ignorant talk of foolish people.

2:16 Live as free people, but do not use your freedom as a cover-up for evil; live as God's slaves.

Peter ONE

Remember the line in *Brave Heart* where William Wallace says, "They may take our lives, but they will never take our freedom!"

We have that type of freedom. We don't always feel free, but by the grace and mercy of our God, we are free. What Peter shares with us is that, because we are free, we should be the best servants ever. We are not slaves by requirement, but we are servants and slaves to the Gospel of Christ, serving him and one another from the love in our heart and not from the stripes on our back.

So, why do so many free men still walk in bondage, trapped in a prison of their own making? Drugs, alcohol, cheating, lying, and porn – these are all prisons from which a free man has been delivered. But it is a choice. We must use our freedom for God's glory, and not to cover up evil deeds. I have known a few of those people who believe that God's grace is enough, and now they can act and do anything they desire. Really, they are right; they can do what they choose, but the rest of the story is that there are consequences to each of their decisions. Let me give you an extreme example.

Let's say that you and I decide to go on a short term mission trip. We plan, we pack, we pray, and so far, so good. We board our plane to a far-off land, and tucked into our suitcases are flyers translated into the local language that introduces people to the Gospel. So far, so good. We land, take a taxi to the downtown area of the city, check in, and decide to go to dinner to get a feel

Peter ONE

for the local culture. Walking out on the street, we know we're not in Kansas anymore.

There are street vendors selling everything from jewelry to drugs, from food to clothing. People recognize we are visitors, and they want our money. As we walk just a few blocks, we see strip clubs, girls on the corner, and a whole culture foreign to us. We know that all this stuff exists, but we are there for the Lord, right? Hey, we are free. We can choose.

Be very careful, my friend. You may say, "Well, Mel, your little story is far-fetched." But is it? Humor me. Finish the story.

Do we turn around, head straight back to our rooms where we may be safe, hit our knees, and pray for all the lost souls we just encountered? Do we formulate a plan on how to get the Gospel to these lost souls? Or are we seduced into the local culture and the evil that is normal here?

The choice is yours. Think about it. What about right where we are? Here in our day-to-day environments, are we compromising the truth? Are we such a part of the local culture that no one knows we are sons and daughters of the Most High God?

When we sin, do we repent at the heart level, or do we just say, "Forgive me Lord," with our head? Trust me, God is not mocked. He knows our heart, and he knows if we truly live for him. He wants us to take the high

Peter ONE

road. We are just visitors here on Earth, passing through on our way to Heaven.

I think it would serve us well to remember that. To take each moment of every day: when we are confronted with a sin choice, we are to choose God's way, his plan, his gory. The ways of sin are death. The ways of righteousness are life. Choose life. Live as free servants of God.

2:17 Show proper respect to everyone, love the family of believers, fear God, honor the emperor.

2:18 Slaves, in reverent fear of God submit yourselves to your masters, not only to those who are good and considerate, but also to those who are harsh.

Peter, these two verses give us a contrast. Show respect to everyone. There are people whom I once respected who have, through their actions, lost respect in my eyes. When men fail to follow through, when they say one thing and do another, respect is lost. We are challenged in so many ways by so many people. The key in these verses is respect, love, and honor.

Respect people for who they are, and for the office they hold. "Love the brotherhood" reminds us that all true Christians form a great family, a family where Father God is the head. Have you ever noticed that some believers get so hung up on denomination that they

Peter ONE

have little to do with a brother or sister across town, let alone around the world? Again, this shows that when man's laws go against God's desires, distortion occurs. We are to love the family of God, not tear it down or speak poorly and in disregard of our brothers.

Then, Peter says to "fear God." It is a phrase that we find throughout the Bible, and it is one of the first duties of a believer. The word "fear," as it is used here, means that we are to revere, honor, and submit to his will. It is that kind of fear, not so much the fear of punishment, suffering, or messing up. Loving God is respecting God to the utmost.

When you were a kid, didn't you seek the approval of your Dad? Sure, we did it, even if he was never around. Even if it seemed we would never get that validation, we wanted it. The same thing holds true with God: we want his approval.

As born-again believers in Jesus, we are brought into this family. The Father loves you, and he wants the very, very best for you.

"*Honor the King*" is a command referring to the authority placed over us. We are to show honor and respect as we live our lives in peace. We need to live in a "no roll" zone. In other words, we do not need to roll our eyes over things that we don't agree with or over people we have a hard time with. We will not always agree with everything, but remember that we carry Christ to a dying world. That world is watching how we respect, how we

Peter ONE

love, how we fear, and how we honor our confession of faith and God. Let's make it our goal to be the best Ambassadors of Christ that we can be. Walk it out in a "no roll" zone.

2:19 For it is commendable if someone bears up under the pain of unjust suffering because they are conscious of God.

2:20 But how is it to your credit if you receive a beating for doing wrong and endure it? But if you suffer for doing good and you endure it, this is commendable before God.

Do we even know what suffering is? Christ was not the first Jewish believer to suffer, and he definitely was not the last. Yes – some people are shocked to discover that Jesus was not a Christian! He, of course, was Jewish, raised in the home of Mary and Joseph, the carpenter. God allowed his son to become man, to be born into a corrupt and dysfunctional world, and to experience the joys and the pains of humanity. Then, he allowed Jesus, his son, to suffer unfairly at the hands of the religious leaders of the day. He allowed his son to die a horrific death on a cross. Unfair suffering beyond what we can imagine for an unworthy, ungrateful, and ungodly world.

You and I have a hero to follow – a model to learn from. Most of our suffering is self-inflicted. We want what we want, and we want it now. Our good and Holy Father knows best that what we want may be not what he

Peter ONE

wants, and when we don't get what we want, we label that suffering! Please. In verse 20, Peter is referring to being beaten for doing wrong, a beating that we have earned. Then, the second part of this verse makes us stop and think about *"suffering doing good,"* which is *commendable before God.*

When was the last time you suffered for doing good? Heck, when was the last time you were even uncomfortable for doing good. The Western Church knows little of true sacrifice or true suffering. When you must hide your Bible in fear for your life, or risk your very life just to attend underground church – that can be classified as suffering.

Currently, there are about 100 million Christians persecuted around the world. There are over 65 countries where Christians are persecuted. North Korea is high on that list, because it is simply illegal to be a Christian there. Estimates are that close to 70,000 North Koreans have been sent to labor camps for their faith. Imagine that. Because you believe in Jesus, you and your family can be arrested and sent away to a labor camp. That is suffering for the truth.

Saudi Arabia, Afghanistan, Iran, Iraq, Somalia, and Ethiopia all made the list, due to radical Islamists. Yes, this sounds crazy. Why can't people just get along? In recent years, we have seen the effects of people who are willing to kill innocent people for their religion.

Peter ONE

We hear of people who will place bombs in crowds and walk away, thinking they have pleased their god! Murder for religion's sake! I would much rather suffer for a cause, in order to reach the world with a message of peace, love, grace, and mercy. This Christian religion that says, "Thou shalt not kill," is a threat to the radical agenda of people who would like to wipe all Jews and Christians off the face of the earth.

I am reminded of the six million Jews who were put to death during the Holocaust. We think we suffer? Hitler was responsible for the death of six million Jews, but he also killed another five million people, just because they disagreed with the politics of the day.

Poles, communists, socialists, slaves, gypsies, the disabled, and more – five million people, plus the six million Jews. Eleven million people were exterminated, because they were considered inferior to the "super race" Hitler was trying to create.

Suffering for God's sake is different from getting what we deserve for our stupid decisions. Suffering? What do we truly know of suffering? Why and how do we handle it when we are the ones who suffer?

2:21 To this you were called, because Christ suffered for you, leaving you an example, that you should his steps.

**2:22 "He committed no sin,
and no deceit was found in his mouth."**

Peter ONE

How are we to follow in these footsteps? The idea in verse 21 is to imitate, to closely walk in the footsteps. When I was a kid, we did not have online games to fill up every waking hour. But we still needed to be entertained, and TV was not to be watched all the time. Yes, we played outside when the weather permitted. But one popular pastime was to "paint by numbers." This was a kit that included a picture with numbers on each area to be painted. In the kit were small containers of paint that were also numbered. The idea was that if you followed the instructions and painted according to the numbers, by the end you would have completed the painting in exact replica of the original.

It seems like horses and clowns were very popular back then. Step by step, number by number, the horse or clown appeared on the painting. Even people without any artistic talent could create a copy of the original.

What Peter is saying to us here is that the kit has been prepared. The original has been produced. Jesus shows us in his Word which numbers to paint, and when we follow the pattern, we can create something that is "suitable for framing."

Let's take verse 22 and paint the picture.

"Commit no sin." "Let no deceit be found in your mouth."

Ok, no sin and no deceit. So, in the paint by number analogy, we would take our brush and place it in the color of righteousness and paint the holy righteousness

Peter ONE

numbers of the picture. Then, we paint truth and honesty in the "no deceit in our mouth" portion of our picture. Peter says to follow in Christ's footsteps. Place your feet right where he has walked, staying in the lines of each section.

We are not just placed at random here on Earth, with no idea and no model to follow. We have been given the model and picture of the best man that has ever walked on Earth. Jesus Christ is his name.

Yes, we read all the teachings that the Son of God gave us, but Peter wants us to look at his actions too.

2:23 When they hurled their insults at him, he did not retaliate; when he suffered, he made no threats. Instead, he entrusted himself to him who judges justly.

When you read this, what emotions does it produce? Think about that, the Lord did not retaliate. It really is a better way to handle the unjust treatment from people. It is for our benefit.

Jesus could have handled it like some would today. But I cannot imagine him saying to Pilate, *"I know we just met, but you need to understand that I am a pretty big deal around here. I have healed the sick, raised the dead, and even made great wine out of a few jugs of water. These religious leaders are threatened by the truth, and that's why they sent me bound to you today. Even though I could call down a whole gang of angels, I*

Peter ONE

will go easy on you if you let me go. Pilate, you need to understand that I am a King, and that my beef is not with you. It's with Annias, and Caiaphas that I will get even. My problem is with the religious leaders from the Temple. They are in big trouble. So, what do you say Pilate? Do we have a deal?"

No, Jesus did not puff himself up. Yes, he is a King, but he allowed himself to be beaten, mocked, and to have a crown of thorns places on his head. He died the death of a common criminal, even though he had committed no crime.

Through it all, he calmly and confidently committed his cause to the *"Judge who judges justly,"* to God the Father.

We are to learn from this. Our Judge is not man, but God. Even if we could lie or cheat our way out of an unjust situation, we must trust God and calmly declare that Jesus is Lord. If he be for me, who can be against me? Let's look at Psalms 37:5-6: "Commit your way to the Lord, trust him and he will do this. He will make your righteous reward shine like the dawn, your vindication like the noonday sun."

Here in 1 Peter, Peter has laid out for us the way to handle insults when people throw them at us. He has showed us how to entrust ourselves to him who judges justly, our Father. Now he is going to challenge us, to give us hope.

Peter ONE

2:24 "He himself bore our sins" in his body on the cross, so that we might die to sins and live for righteousness; "by his wounds you have been healed."

Read that again! "He himself bore our sins in his body." Our God is so good that he allowed our sins to be placed on the body of Christ. There are no words written that can ever express how the absolute worst was bore in the body of an absolutely undeserving man, yet our Savior took them all with him to the cross. It was a horrifying death he chose to die for us. The sin of the world, your sin and my sin, hung there on that tree so that we could die to it.

Then, he tells us why. It is not that we are good and do not ourselves deserve to be put to death. It was so that we may live. Our sins in Him on the cross meant our death to sin. It frees us from sin to walk in righteousness. It gives us life. Don't miss that point. He allowed our sin to be placed on him to die with him. Then, he allowed his life, his resurrection life, to be placed in us so that we may live. It's the great exchange. We will never make a better deal than that, no matter how long we live. Most of us want to get a good deal on buying a house or a car.

I have even met people who brag how they have bought and sold and have never come out on the short end of any transaction. But this spiritual transaction with God will never be topped. You have heard, "We want a win-win deal," right? Well, how does Jesus win? By taking

Peter ONE

our sin and dying? We win big time. Remember, it is our sin. We deserved death. We win! We are allowed to take new life and walk in righteousness. We win again. We are forever pardoned by the work on the cross, set free to go and sin no more. We win.

Then he goes on to say, "By his wounds you have been healed." Have been. Past tense. Have been healed. From the inside out, we have been healed. Part of walking in righteousness is justification, and the only way we are justified is through Jesus. His people, you and I, receive righteousness through faith in Jesus alone. For it is Jesus who is the Christ, the sinless Son of God who took humanity's sins upon himself to become the Lamb of God. He was offered up for you and I! We win, and when we come back to God, he wins. He redeemed us, and he restores us back to fellowship with him, in order to be his people. Healed from sin and made whole again – body, mind, and spirit.

Peter is referring to Isaiah 53:4-6. The prophet predicted the coming of Christ. Peter would have been very familiar with the writings of Isaiah. The book of Isaiah has been referred to as "The Book of Salvation." The name Isaiah means "The Lord is Salvation." It's no surprise that many Jews read and became very familiar with each book of the Old Testament, or the Tanakh.

Of course, most of us have heard of the Torah, which represents the Jewish Bible. Tanakh is comprised of three subdivisions. The Torah (teaching, also known as the five books of Moses), the Nevi'im (prophets), and

Peter ONE

the Ketuxim (writings). Three parts that made up one. God's design. Three in one – Father, Son, and Holy Spirit.

I have discovered over the years that if you look, you will find that the gospel and trinity are ever present. Have you ever noticed that? So, Jesus bore our sins in his body on the cross so that we might die to sin and live for him. But do we get it? Peter goes on to say:

2:25 For "you were like sheep going astray," but now you have returned to the Shepherd and Overseer of your souls.

Sheep gone astray – that's *"baaaad"*. Seriously, when Peter shares these comments, don't you see the picture of a flock without a shepherd? I do. And sheep that have no overseer or protector will wander and meander without direction. Many will scatter and follow their own path, a path that very well could lead to destruction. I was a lost sheep, wandering meaninglessly, until I heard the voice of the true shepherd.

Peter is referring to a whole people group, a group of people who were following nothing but selfish and evil desires. They were a people who, through a great and wonderful plan of Salvation, were recovered from a sad life without a true flock or leader.

Jesus is the overseer, or bishop, of our souls. Not only do we come back to the safety of the flock, but we also come to the true leadership of God. He watches over

Peter ONE

you and I, and he takes special interest in providing a safe place for our soul. Our soul is entrusted to the great shepherd, the overseer, and it is safer than precious gold in a vault. We are forever His, and we are forever safe, unless we choose to leave the safety of the flock and shepherd.

Unfortunately, I have seen people do that, deciding that they are better off doing things on their own and going their own way. They miss a few Sundays, thinking they will have more time to get stuff done or thinking they can be fed through televangelism. I enjoy a great message on TV as much as anyone, but it was never meant to replace a local flock that gathers together, prays together, and shares each others' victories and pains.

As great as it would be, the TV can't give you a hug. Does that make sense? We belong to God, and he will never let us go. But if we choose to let go and stray away, heaven help us.

Wrapping up his second chapter, Peter encourages us to return to the safe and wonderful shepherd, to stay in the safety of the flock of the overseer of our soul. Let us commit ourselves to him, resolving to wander no more. Let us keep in the safety he provides and follow the leading of our great shepherd, Jesus.

We have seen firsthand the pain and the unhappiness that living for ourselves produces. We have seen that we need a savior and that God, in his glory and wisdom, provided his only Son to save a dying world. We have

Peter ONE

seen that, by accepting our Lord, we were changed forever. We were redeemed and made whole. Our names are written in the Book of Life.

We have seen and felt the safety of God, his Son, and his Holy Spirit. So, the question is: why would we ever leave this safe place? Why would Adam and Eve risk the safety of the garden and the wonderful fellowship of the Father? It doesn't make sense. But sin came as a result of the fall of man. Sin can sound good, but it never makes spiritual sense.

Wives and Husbands

3:1 Wives, in the same way submit yourselves to your own husbands so that, if any of them do not believe the word, they may be won over without words by the behavior of their wives,

3:2 when they see the purity and reverence of your lives.

We live in a sensitive, politically correct, and victim-focused world. There are things from the Word of God that some people cannot handle, because it interferes with how they want to live their lives. As followers of Christ, why would we want to run our lives? I mean, out of our own strength and knowledge. Why would we want to do this, when we can rely on Him?

Peter ONE

Peter 3:1 is one of those statements that drives some people nuts. Make this comment today, and the PC police are out in full-force, ready to unleash attacks on you, your God, your family, and your friends. All because you dare to speak the Word as it was written. But let's take a closer look.

In verse 1, when he says "In the same way," he must be referring to what he just wrote. Looking back at the final verse in 2:25, we see we were like sheep gone astray. But then we returned to the shepherd, the overseer of our soul. Then, he starts by teaching wives to be submissive to their husbands in the same way. A shepherd loves and protects his flock.

Ephesians 5:25 reads: *"Husbands love your wives even as Christ also loved the church and give himself up for her."*

A shepherd must be willing to put himself at risk to protect his sheep. A husband must love and protect his wife, too. Many times in this fallen world, that is not the case. The mentality seems to be every man for himself. Many men seem to be less honorable than expected. They appear to be "unfollowable." Why would any woman want to follow a man like that? Why would she want to submit to a husband who does not believe, who does not walk with integrity, and who lives his life with the idea that it is all about him?

Let's discuss the thought behind Peter's comment here. It's a teaching moment, if you will. Before man was

Peter ONE

created, there existed the Lord Jesus. Yes, you read that right. God the Father, Jesus the Son, and the Holy Spirit, together known as the Holy Trinity, existed in the heavenly realm. When God created mankind, this pattern was followed. We see Adam, Eve, and Children. Three in one family. Father-Son-Holy Spirit. Husband-Wife-Children. God-Pastor-Church. Owner-Boss-Worker.

Do you see the pattern, the design of God, everywhere you look? Do you see how submission is built into this design? Of course it is. Jesus said he did nothing but the will of the Father who sent him. He was submissive to a good and loving Father.

Wives, submit to your husbands. Pastor, submit to your God and flock. And so it goes. Godly submission is as natural as breathing, when you know that the person you are submitting to has submitted to the Lord. Submit to the submitted, does that help?

In the same way, when people see our beautiful submission to God, they may come to the conclusion that they need that type of relationship to surrender to. Peter is saying, "Let your family see the purity and reverence of your life. They will want that too!" So much so, that wives may win over unsaved husbands.

3:3 Your beauty should not come from outward adornment, such as elaborate hairstyles and the wearing of gold jewelry or fine clothes.

Peter ONE

Released in 1984, there was a song by Madonna called "Material Girl". (Robert Rans, Perter Brown; Copyright 1982 Sony/ATV Songs, LLC)

It put her on the map. The lyrics, of course, identify with an affluent life rather than a life with deep relationships. *"Living in a material world, and I am a material girl. You know that we are living in a material world, and I am a material girl."* The success of the song was partially because it hit close to the truth! Unfortunately, many people place too great an importance on how they look, what they wear, what they drive, and the neighborhood in which they live.

Materialism has taken these good people down a road on which it is hard to find a place to make a u-turn. When some people get a taste of the "good life," they can't stop eating, and they eventually become gluttons. Others get a taste of the Lord Jesus and discover the "God Life," knowing that it is all about how we can bring him glory. The more we partake, the healthier we become. So, we have a choice. We can choose to walk in a healthy relationship with Christ, or we can choose the outward appearance over the inner man.

Peter has us focus on the inner beauty of our spiritual health, and not the outward appearance of hair and jewelry. That's easy, right? Well, in this material world, with ad after ad on TV, in magazines, or the radio – all of them doing their best to get us to buy the latest weight loss secret or the coolest fashion – We must keep our spirits built up, knowing that we need to focus on the inside beauty. The outward will of course follow.

Peter ONE

Recently a friend of mine we had scheduled to speak to a group of guys made the following statement, *"It is not about the cars, the cash, or the cottages, it's about the cause."* I like that. Materialism is very temporary; the cause of Christ is eternal.

3:4 Rather, it should be that of your inner self, the unfading beauty of a gentle and quiet spirit, which is of great worth in God's sigh sight.

There you go. Peter says to focus on the inner man, the part that is concealed to the natural eye, and not on the appearance of braided hair, fine clothes, or gold jewelry. None of that really matters. The ornament of a meek and quiet spirit, a gentle disposition, or a loving smile that starts with a heart given to God is so much more beautiful than any gold placed on a finger or wrapped around the neck

Let me say this: Do I appreciate my wife looking great? Yes, I do, but I don't see the outward as much as I do the inner woman. Our hearts are connected, and she is always beautiful to me. Diamonds or no diamonds, gold or no gold, she sparkles brighter than diamonds and is of greater value than gold. I know she loves the Lord. She has a good heart, and she would do anything to help people in need. I have seen it, and it is awesome to behold. I think this is what Peter is referring to.

I may not see the difference between silver or white gold, glass or diamonds, or fake nails or the real ones. But I can see and appreciate a gentle heart seeking

Peter ONE

after God. A quiet confidence that grows out of time spent in the Bible and in prayer. These are real, and, believe me, they are much more valuable than any gold or silver.

3:5 For this is the way the Holy women of the past who put their hope in God used to make themselves beautiful. They were submissive to their own husbands.

3:6 Like Sarah, who obeyed Abraham and called him her master. You are daughters if you do what is right and do not give away to fear.

Peter uses historical women of faith to communicate truth. A woman who puts her hope in a loving Father, who calls her "my daughter," is beautiful. She is beautiful from the inside-out. She is submissive in a good way, fulfilling God's design for marriage.

The disciples were submissive to Christ Jesus, the Son of God. Jesus was submissive to God the Father.

In the military it is known as the chain of command. A commissioned officer will gain the salute of the soldier or seaman, and those of higher rank will be addressed as "Sir." I can still hear, "Sir, yes, Sir," ringing in the recesses of my mind. In the Navy there are Master Chiefs, and in the Army there are Master Sergeants. In the Army of God, we have but one Master, Jesus Christ. So when Peter writes in verse six, "Sarah, who obeyed Abraham and called him Master," he did it as an

Peter ONE

example of submission. Remember, the disciples were submissive to the Lord, and they called him Master.

Submission really was God's idea, and it was also God's idea to give us free well to choose to submit. We freely show respect, or not. But blessing follows those who follow God's model. Those who submit their wills, as Christ did, to the Father will share in the blessings of the Kingdom of God. Speaking of God's Kingdom and his design: men, you are not off the hook.

3:7 Husbands, in the same way be considerate as you live with your wives, and treat them with respect as the weaker partner and as heirs with you of the gracious gift of life, so that nothing will hinder your prayers.

Men, we are to love our wives. In Ephesians 5:25, we read, *"Husbands, love your wives, as Christ loved the church and gave himself for her."* Just before that, we read in Ephesians 5:21, *"Submit to one another out of reverence for Christ."*

I like the "Instructions for Christian Households" title that was placed in that portion of Scripture in the NIV, for two reasons. First, it really does communicate to the reader what we are supposed to get from that section of Scripture. Secondly, the important thing is that we read and understand the Holy Bible, and the section in 1 Peter we are discussing may be one of the most misunderstood messages of the day.

Peter ONE

What is all of this talk of submission for wives and husbands? What is Peter trying to communicate to men when he says, "Be considerate," or when he says not to let anything "hinder our prayers."

Throughout history, up to this point, wives were considered to be not much more than slaves. They were like personal property, regarded with little honor or respect. But when Peter said to be considerate, meaning to honor them, he speaks truth. It's not just because they are more delicate, or not as physically strong; it's that this new and improved man sees his wife as a helper, alongside him through highs and lows. She is a wonderful partner in life, but not a slave, as some cultures view women.

We agree that, of course, a husband should honor his wife, and, of course, a wife should respect her husband. But with current divorce rates running at about 50%, and with families being torn apart like a sheet of paper, you wouldn't guess it.

You can tear the paper, and what you have in either hand is a piece of the whole. When God does the making of marriage, it is forever. It is for good. He puts a man and woman together for his glory. He created marriage when he created Adam and Eve.

Like waiting for the ice to get thick enough to skate on, at the beginning of winter, men and women must be patient with each other for great things to happen in marriage. Mutual respect and honor goes a long way.

Peter ONE

My wife and I have been married for over thirty years. We have survived the process of blessing our family together. The road has had some twists and turns and some bumps, but we have made it this far by trusting in God's wisdom of putting two broken lives together to create something special.

I can't count the number of times early on when I said, "God put us together and will keep us together." Believing in the wisdom and love of our Heavenly Father, over the years – through mutual respect – we have grown closer and closer still. It takes two!

As a husband, let me encourage you to honor and cherish your wife. She is a gift from God in your life. What you build together while here on earth, and the spiritual bond you create by seeking, submitting to, and honoring God, can be a beautiful legacy for your children, grandchildren, and generations to come. You do not want anything to hinder your prayers!

Suffering for Doing Good

3:8 Finally, all of you, be like-minded, be sympathetic, love one another, be compassionate and humble.

When Peter says this, he is making sure we are all included. He first addressed the wives and husbands, and now he is speaking to all believers. He delivers a wonderful request. I would say it this way: "Ok, all of you, can't we just get along?" But he tells you and I to

Peter ONE

live in harmony, meaning that we should live in agreement as one.

Here is a thought: if we are the Body of Christ, the Family of Believers, when do we start acting like it? When do we stand as one for what's right? I have always heard that there is strength in numbers, and if the Body of Christ would work together, much would be accomplished. It almost seems we are more concerned with the name above the door or the church building than we are with the people inside.

What is important is what is inside each believer's heart, not the labels or denominations we seem to have to use. You and I belong to the Lord Jesus, no matter what denomination we call ourselves. Church, "live in harmony," sounds great, but there is so much competition and jealousy between the "churches" in most cities that it's difficult to see the harmony. And of course that is what the "world" sees in regards to the church. "They cannot even get along with each other, why would I want to be a part of that mess."

Peter encourages us to be of one mind, the mind of Christ. We are to show sympathy and empathy for each other. To love as brothers, we need to enter into one another's feelings, care for each other, and share the joy and the pain of each other's lives. Love as families love, for we are the family of God.

He then goes on. Be compassionate and humble. I can hear it now – great, you mean we are to be all these

Peter ONE

things to each other? I thought we were to treat everyone like family! There is the issue. In today's world, it is a sad commentary, when we show more respect, more love, and more compassion toward co-workers or strangers than we do our own families.

As believers, this should not be. We must train ourselves to show all these things and more. Remember we carry Christ in us, the hope of glory. I dare say that if we were walking in harmony as the church, if we were all standing against the injustice of the disintegration of the family, things would change.

If we took each other's hand and took a stand, things would change. We must stop fighting each other, and we must fight the good fight of faith. Only then can we make a difference.

3:9 Do not repay evil with evil or insult with insult. On the contrary, repay evil with blessing, because to this you were called so that you may inherit a blessing.

What a concept. Do not get even. Do not have the last word. No more "don't get mad, get even." Isn't this how the world thinks? Isn't this how we have been taught to respond? Yes, but what Peter points out to us is that there is a Christ like response to every circumstance.

When someone does something or says something to hurt us, it usually does hurt. But if we retaliate and try to one-up them, all we are doing is making matters worse.

Peter ONE

This Godly response will produce the fruit of peace, rather than anger or bitterness.

Jesus makes this point in Matthew 5:43-44: *"You have heard it was said, love your neighbor and hate your enemy; but I tell you; love your enemies and pray for those who persecute you."* Look, do you want more human nature, or do you want more of God's nature filling your life? Of course, we want more of God, so why is this concept of repaying insult with blessing so difficult for most?

I think the key is found not in just the words of Jesus, but in his actions here on Earth. When he was arrested, falsely accused, sentenced to die, and hung on a cross, that, my friend, was unfair. But what was his response? How did he repay the people who put him there on that cross? Yes, the Jewish leaders were there, the Roman soldiers were there, and the onlookers in the crowd who were the first to yell out, "Crucify him," were there.

All had a part in putting the Lord Jesus on that cross. But so did I, and so did you. We had a part, because Jesus went to the cross for all of us, to redeem us from the curse of the law and to give us a new and better life. He gave us a way back to the heart of God. He paid the price that we owed, and he set us free to live a life that honors him. Yes, the Jewish leaders and the Romans were enemies of the truth. But so were you and I.

And what was our punishment for our sin that deserved death? Luke 23:34: *"Jesus said, 'Father, forgive them,*

Peter ONE

for they do not know what they are doing.'" Forgive them. He could have called on a heavenly army to strike each and every one of us down. It's what we deserved.

Instead, even in death, our Lord Jesus was showing us a better way. Forgive. As followers of Christ, we are to live a life of blessing and forgiveness. We have been given a blessing, and it is so much more that the word has to offer. Now, as a blessed people, we need to be ready to scatter blessings and forgiveness to others. Remember not to bless just your friends and families, but also your enemies.

Be ready to take the criticism and unjust treatment, bear it and not respond in like manner. Give back blessing, give back prayer, even wish them well, in Christ. Keep in mind they need the hope of salvation, as much as you and I.

Be ready to take a stand for your faith. Of course, too many times we have, as the Church, simply gone along and ended up with laws that are contrary to God's law. Abortion laws come to mind. We did not stand up for righteousness back in the 70's, and we continue to allow the deaths of thousands of helpless, innocent babies every day. But do we pray that this bad law be reversed? Do we actually pray that the doctors and staff at the abortion clinics across our nation and around the world repent and find the truth in Christ? Do we pray they discover that every life is precious, that every person not yet born has a right to life?

Peter ONE

Be ready with your Godly response in an ungodly world. It is when we scatter blessings that people will see in us something different – something better – and will want what we have! It is contrary to the world's ways to repay insult with blessing, but it is a much better way. It's Christ in you that makes this happen.

**3:10 For Whoever would love life
   and see good days
must keep their tongue from evil
   and their lips from deceitful speech.**

**3:11 They must turn from evil and do good;
   they must seek peace and pursue it.**

**3:12 For the eyes of the Lord are on the righteous and his ears are attentive to their prayer,
but the face of the Lord is against those who do evil.**

Peter quotes Psalm 34:12-16 here to make his point to not repay evil with evil. He emphasizes that we be a blessing. Had he included 34:11, it would have started it this way: *"Come, my children, listen to me; I will teach you the fear of the Lord."*

Many times, that is the key to learning the things of God. To come as children and to listen, as if our very lives depend on it. Because wouldn't you agree that our quality of life absolutely depends on listening?. *"Faith*

Peter ONE

comes by hearing the message, and the message is heard through the word of Christ" (Romans 10:17).

When we come as children to listen, we love life with abandon. We must keep this excitement and enthusiasm as we grow. Years ago in my seminars, I made the observation of how excited kids can be. I mean, everything is great when you're a kid! Then, life pressures seem to wear down our positive outlooks, and they take the edge off of our enthusiasm. What happens? Sometimes, kids have high energy, and if they are too excited we squelch them either with drugs or with our idea of what acceptable behavior is in children.

It is almost as if we are saying to them, "Sit down, shut up, and be boring like me." Ouch, the truth sometimes stings.

Peter quotes the Psalms, so that people of this day may be reminded to love life and to see good days. Keep your tongue from evil, and keep your mouth from deceitful speech. Very, very wise words indeed. Love life, keep positive, and speak words of encouragement, rather than destructive speech. He then continues and hits the nail on the head by finishing with the following points: *"turn from sin to do good, and seek peace and pursue it."*

The next verse should encourage all of us. *"The eyes of the Lord are on the righteous."* Peter and the Psalms

Peter ONE

are reminding us of a truth in our relationship with our Father.

Father God must look upon the righteous. Think of it this way: without Christ, we have no hope. Through his blood and his work on the cross, we are restored to fellowship with the Father. We can be seen as part of the family. We have no righteousness – none, except through and in Christ Jesus.

Only there can we expect to have our Father's attention. There, he can place his eyes upon us, and his ears are attentive to our prayers. There, in the secret place of the most high. There, so many want to dwell, to stay in the shadow of our Loving God.

So why is it so difficult to stay in this place?

Why do we ever walk out of righteousness and expose ourselves to the attacks of our enemy? Because we are but mere men, you say? Yes, that is true; but there is nothing mere about our God or his Son Jesus. The "mere" Savior of the world? That is where our identity must be found, if we are ever to have his eyes and ears on us.

3:13 Who is going to harm you if you are eager to do good?

Who? A world in which everything has been turned upside down is one that will set out to destroy the good things of God. But Peter is saying to be eager to do

Peter ONE

good, for the sake of him who sent you. Even if evil finds its way to your door, you are protected.

In Psalms 37:1-6, we read:

Do not fret because of those who are evil
or be envious of those who do wrong;
for like the grass they will soon wither,
like green plants they will soon die away.

Trust in the LORD and do good;
dwell in the land and enjoy safe pasture.
Take delight in the LORD,
and he will give you the desires of your heart.

Commit your way to the LORD;
trust in him and he will do this:
He will make your righteous reward shine like the dawn,
your vindication like the noonday sun.

We are fully aware that evil exists. We know the cosmic battle has been raging since the fall of man, and this battle is fought day by day by people who are eager to do good and people who are willing to do evil.

Being a follower of Christ does not mean that we have absolute security, but it does mean that we have eternal security.

Recently, we watched *End of the Spear*, a 2006 movie that portrays the real-life events of a group of Christian

Peter ONE

missionaries who attempted to evangelize the Huaorani People of the Jungle of Ecuador.

Most people think it was a movie about Jim Elliot, and, while his story is best known, there were five other male missionaries who died that day in 1956. This film tells its story from the perspective of Steve "Stevie" Saint. He was the son of Nate Saint, one of the murdered missionaries. If you get an opportunity to rent the movie, do it. You will not be disappointed. Here was a group of committed families that wanted to take the gospel to a tribe of people who had no contact with the outside world. They paid the price not only of giving up some of the comforts of home, but of their very lives.

Who is going to harm you, if you are eager to do good? Let yourself be eager to do good, to do kingdom work and be put into motion, and most likely you will find out!

Peter is reassuring us to stay the course, to do good, and to live holy and pure lives in Christ. Then, as the cruel and unjust world does its best to bring you down, know that the victory belongs to the Lord.

Our witness in how we handle the world is how people are drawn to Christ. Our peace and joy are found in Christ alone, so we must remain eager to do good and to trust our Father with the outcome.

3:14 But even if you should suffer for what is right, you are blessed. "Do not fear their threats; do not be frightened."

Peter ONE

In other words, if you suffer for righteousness' sake, be blessed. When things don't go your way, be blessed. When all hell is breaking loose against you, be blessed. Sure, it doesn't feel like a blessing in the midst of the storms of life, but we are a blessed people who can confidently say, "I know my Jesus, and he knows my future. No matter the present pain or past failures, I am blessed of God through Jesus Christ."

Don't be afraid of what everyone else fears. What does man fear? Well, a few things come to mind. What I would like you to see is that, in Christ, these fears lose their power.

Fear: *So do not fear, for I am with you;*
  do not be dismayed, for I am your God.
I will strengthen you and help you;
  I will uphold you with my righteous right hand.
(Isaiah 41:10)

Fear of Death: *Eternal Life in Christ* (John 3:16).

Fear of Failure: *I can do all this through him who gives me strength* (Philippians 4:13)

Fear of Condemnation: *Therefore, there is no condemnation for those who are in Christ Jesus.* (Romans 8:1)

Fear of Future: *I know the plans I have for you, declares the Lord* (Jeremiah 29:11).

Peter ONE

Fear of Pain: *He will wipe every tear from their eyes. There will be no more death or mourning or crying or pain, for the old order of things has passed away."* (Revelation 21:4)

Fear of Grief: *So with you: Now is your time of grief, but I will see you again and you will rejoice, and no one will take away your joy.* (John 16:22)

Fear of Trouble: *Blessed is the man who always fears the LORD, but he who hardens his heart falls into trouble.* (Proverbs 28:14)

3:15 But in your hearts revere Christ as Lord. Always be prepared to give an answer to everyone who asks you to give the reason for the hope that you have. But do this with gentleness and respect, keeping a clear conscience, so that those who speak maliciously against your good behavior in Christ may be ashamed of their slander.

If our hearts are "set apart" in Christ, we have hope. We are moving and being in eternal hope. The God of grace and mercy lives in us and we in him. Of course, we have hope. In Christ our hope is well placed, and it is made complete. When asked, we can respond from a full heart – a heart sanctified in Christ.

Have you ever had someone say, "There is something different about you," or, "Why are you are so happy all

Peter ONE

the time?" People see your joy when you are in Christ, as much as they saw your human nature before you came to know him.

When they ask, we need to be prepared to give an answer. Over the years, I have trained people in business to be able to give an "elevator" speech. It communicates who they are and what they do in a very short and concise manner. About the amount of time it takes an elevator to go from the ground floor to the fifth floor.

You never know who you will run into or how important it will be to be able to lay out your mission, your value proposition, or your goods or services in a concise manner.

Let me give you an example of someone who sells real estate. When asked what you do, you may respond, "Oh I sell houses." But, if you want to make an impact, you could say, "I am so glad that you asked. I help people obtain the American dream. I help people find a home to raise their family in. It is such a great job, every day I get to help people obtain assets and dreams."

Do you see the difference? So, where Peter is telling us to be prepared to give an answer for why we have hope, let's take this idea of an elevator speech and respond in a gentle, but concise, way. If someone at school, work, or the grocery store asks, "Why are you so happy?" What is our response? Or if they ask, "Are you one of those, you know, Christians?" You might say, "Yes, I'm

Peter ONE

a Christian." Or you could say, "I'm so glad that you asked. Yes, I am a follower of Christ. I learned over the years that living for myself was shallow, and it seemed like all I did was go from one mess to another. But a few years ago, I gave my life to Christ, and it was a game changer. I now have purpose, joy, and a hope and a future that are bright."

Be ready in season and out of season to give an answer for the reason you have hope. This fallen world has no hope, and it needs to know where the true source of all hope is found. You may be the only person who gets the chance to share the good news with that person. Be ready with a clear message of hope.

Live your faith out loud. Be consistent, be of good courage, and know that he who brought you here will never abandon you, and the people who slander the name of Christ in you will be put to shame because of your faith.

3:17 For it is better, if it is God's will, to suffer for doing good than for doing evil.

In a brief conversation with a neighbor the other day, my neighbor stated that his girlfriend left him and moved out! Of course, I was a bit taken aback. I had thought she was his wife. But I tried to not look shocked. I asked what reason she would have to do that. He said, "Well, she found out that she had breast cancer, and she moved to Texas to be close to family." He then made it clear that he loves her, and he hopes she comes back.

Peter ONE

All of this took place as we unloaded his new 72-inch TV. I guess we all find ways to cope with life's ups and downs. We all have our ways of trying to get through the difficult times. He confessed that he is a recovering alcoholic, so if you think about the choices he could have made to cope with the pain, I guess that purchasing a big TV is better than a big bottle of booze.

Suffering is not uncommon. For a believer, it is part of the process. It's not a matter of if we suffer; it's a matter of how we suffer. Do we drown the suffering with drink? Do we go buy the biggest TV in the store? Or do we rejoice in the Lord, that he would count us worthy to suffer for his will?

Peter reminds us that we can suffer for doing evil, and of course we should. But when we suffer for doing God's will, it is good to realize that there is a purpose to the suffering. Picture this: you are standing before a judge, accused of a crime you did not commit. The arrest was made using eyewitness accounts of your crime. The Judge, after a few questions, looks at the Prosecutor and asks, "Are you sure this man has committed this crime?" The answer comes back, "Yes, Your Honor, we have people who will testify that they saw him commit the crime." So, the Judge pronounces you guilty for a crime you did not commit. Then, he sentences you to ten years of hard labor!

The Prosecutor speaks up and gets everyone in the courtroom to speak out against you! "That's not good enough. This person needs to die for what they have

Peter ONE

done." Now, remember that you are innocent. You know that these people are lying. You know that 10 years of hard labor could be a death sentence, but you trust the system. You think there is a purpose for what is happening. There must be.

Then, the Judge speaks up, quiets the courtroom, and says, "On second thought, you shall die for your crime!" You will be put to death today! No appeal, no delay. In chains, they lead you out to suffer and die for a crime you did not commit.

What are you thinking as you read this? There's no way that could happen – not in our justice system. Of course, what we just saw was the trial of Christ. He was innocent, and we are not. He was condemned, and we should have been. He suffered humiliation, when we could have. He died on the cross, where we should have. He rose from the grave, and we can too! He conquered sin and death so that we may live and have life to the fullest!

Yes, bad things happen to good people. We need to rejoice when we suffer for Christ's sake. But if the suffering is brought on by committing a crime, of our own stupid accord, then so be it. If we are to suffer, let it be by the hand of God. It is in suffering that most of us grow the most. It is there that our flesh seems weak, but that our God seems so strong. It is there that we throw ourselves at the mercy of the court, and Jesus steps in as our advocate to say, "I have already paid the price,

Peter ONE

and this person is forgiven, set him free", then he looks us in the eye and says, "go and sin no more."

3:18 For Christ also suffered once for sins, the righteous for the unrighteous, to bring you to God. He was put to death in the body but made alive in the Spirit.

There it is: the gospel, plain and simple. God loved us so much that he allowed his one and only Son to suffer and die for our sins. No matter if we were good in our own eyes, we were all sinners in his eyes, and he wanted so much to restore our relationship to himself that he sent his Son to Earth. Jesus came to die on a cross. He came as a gift from God the Father to all men, to make a way of escape from sin and certain death. He came to show us a better way to love, a better way to serve, and a better way to live.

Jesus came as man, he lived as man, he taught all men, he walked with men, he ate with sinners, he laughed and cried with humanity, as he still does today.

Peter writes, *"Christ died for sins, once and for all."* We need to realize that it was once and for all. Jesus, the Lamb of God, takes away the sin of the world. The righteous for the unrighteous! His righteousness in exchange for our unrighteous mess. It is not a fair trade, but it is one that shows love, grace, and mercy. The purpose is "to bring us back to God." To restore the intended relationship with the Father, Christ died for us in his physical body, but he was made alive by the spirit.

Peter ONE

3:19 After being made alive, he went and made proclamation to the imprisoned spirits—

3:20-21 to those who were disobedient long ago when God waited patiently in the days of Noah while the ark was being built. In it only a few people, eight in all, were saved through water,

(21) and this water symbolizes baptism that now saves you also—not the removal of dirt from the body but the pledge of a clear conscience toward God. It saves you by the resurrection of Jesus Christ...

3:22 who has gone into heaven and is at God's right hand—with angels, authorities and powers in submission to him

There have been several lines of thought regarding verse 19.

I grew up a heathen. Seriously, I know I was, and my brothers and sisters were, too. My Mom, when she had had enough of our rambunctious activity, would say something like, "You're a bunch of heathens! Sit down, and not another word!" Or she would say, "Quiet, you heathens! I'm trying to think." Of course, she loved her children, and when I analyze her statements I find truth in them.

Peter ONE

Before I was saved, before I was part of the Family of God, I was a heathen. So were the people in the days of Noah. From the fall of man in Genesis 3 to the great flood in Genesis 6, a lot transpired. Men and women started wearing clothes made by God (Genesis 3:21), mankind was kicked out of the Garden of Eden, and people started having kids.

Adam was 130 years old when he had a son and named him Seth. In his younger years, Adam and his wife, Eve, had given birth to a son whose was Cain. Later, they gave birth to another son and named him Abel.

Now, remember that this was after the fall. As we could imagine, these boys were heathen kids – so much so that Cain ended up killing his brother Abel, because Cain was jealous. Cain, filled with envy and anger, took his own brother's life (Genesis 4).

Heathen people existed early on in the history of man. They were people who allowed the desires of a new world overcome their own good judgment. In those days, men would sometimes live to be 800-900 years old! Methuselah actually lived to a ripe old age of 969 years old before he died.

There are days when I wish I could live that long, but then I think, "Wait a minute. The longer I am here on earth, the shorter I will have in Heaven." I'm not in a rush to get there, because if we are alive today, it must mean that God has a purpose for our lives. We might as well make the very best Kingdom decisions that we can.

Peter ONE

Some believe that Jesus, while in the tomb after his death, raided Hell and took back the keys of death from the enemy. Some believe he preached and set the captive free. For years, I have been taught that. In verse 19, we read, "He preached to the spirits in prison," and in verse 20 they are characterized as those "who disobeyed long ago when God waited patiently."

So, Christ preached to the spirits who disobeyed God. That could refer to all who were born and who have died since the fall of man. But there is a group of heathens singled out here in this text: the group of people who did not repent when given the chance, when God destroyed the world with a great flood.

Noah and his family were saved, but the people who died without repentance received a chance to hear the Son of God in the spiritual realm. Can you imagine the chains that held them in prison, the lack of hope, and the realization that this is the sentence for dying without God? Then, his Son shows up "to set the captive free."

Why would he preach to just this one group that disobeyed God before the flood? What about the rest? The real question is: Is he talking to you today? Is he preaching the good news still today, and are we listening to the life-saving message of God's love today?

I am not saying we need to deeply analyze and try to figure the exact time, place, and people Jesus preached to; but to rather, know the message of love,

Peter ONE

grace, mercy, repentance, obedience, and salvation that sets us all free from the prison of sin.

The acceptance of Jesus, the Son of God, releases a person from bondage, and it fulfills the mission statement of Jesus. His mission statement, you may ask? Yes, let's look at Luke 4:18-19:

> [18] *"The Spirit of the Lord is on me,*
> *because he has anointed me*
> *to proclaim good news to the poor.*
> *He has sent me to proclaim freedom for the prisoners*
> *and recovery of sight for the blind,*
> *to set the oppressed free*
>
> [19] *to proclaim the year of the Lord's favor."*

When given the chance, Jesus "preached" his first message from Isaiah 61. Then, he said, *"Today this scripture is fulfilled in your hearing."*

He is still preaching this message to the spirits in prison. The spirits that need to be set free, our blind eyes that need to be opened so that we may see the Kingdom of Heaven, our oppression that must be broken, and our hearts and minds need this year of the Lord's favor.

Listen, my dear friend, God never wanted his people to walk in sin. We chose it. He wants us to experience the wonderful freedom in Christ Jesus. It is the enemy who wants us to keep quiet about the things of God. It is

Peter ONE

Satan who wants to keep us locked up in prison and despair. To our enemy, we say, "No!"

Satan, you are a liar and the Father of lies. We are set free in Christ, and we walk in that freedom. Someone once said, "Freedom is never free." That is true enough, but our freedom was paid for on a cross over two thousand years ago. The price was paid for your freedom. My question is: what are you doing with this gift? Are you walking around defeated, or are you fulfilling the mission statement of Jesus? You are free. Start acting like it. Better yet, don't just act like it. Live your freedom in Christ Jesus!

When Peter writes that people were saved through water, he writes of the eight who were on the Ark. But then he says, *"This water symbolizes baptism that now saves you also. Not the removal of dirt from the body but the pledge of good conscience toward God."*

Think of it this way: no one can be saved without a regenerated and purified heart. Baptism is an appropriate symbol of being saved, and when someone is baptized we see the picture of the old man going under the water to come up a new person. It is done in the name of the Father, Son, and Holy Spirit.

Peter, using the story of Noah, shows how water destroyed the Earth and everything in it, except for eight people. Noah, a righteous man, and his family were saved. I have even read that Noah was "saved by water," as Peter uses that analogy here. But was it the

Peter ONE

water that saved Noah, or was it the Ark? Water destroyed and purged the earth of people who had become wicked.

In **Genesis 6:5 &7**, we read:

"The LORD saw how great the wickedness of the human race had become on the earth, and that every inclination of the thoughts of the human heart was only evil all the time. ⁶ The LORD regretted that he had made human beings on the earth, and his heart was deeply troubled. ⁷ So the LORD said, "I will wipe from the face of the earth the human race I have created—and with them the animals, the birds and the creatures that move along the ground—for I regret that I have made them."

When he said *'I will wipe mankind whom I have created, from the face of the earth"* He meant it.

And he did it! The flood destroyed evil, but God started over with one righteous family, which was saved on the Ark. So, here is the picture: the flood wipes out evil, and the Ark saves God's seed. Eight people are used to restore man to Earth. Again, I ask the question: was it the flood or the Ark that saved?

Well, the way I see it, it was neither. What saved Noah was obedience. When God said to build an Ark to exact dimensions, Noah might have said, "Lord, I have never built anything with my hands, let alone a 450-feet long, 75-feet wide, and 45-feet tall boat. Don't you have someone who works with wood, someone more

Peter ONE

qualified?" But he walked with God. When you walk with God, you talk with God, and he may ask things of you that will move you out of your comfort zone. Actually, that's normally when you know it is God. Chances are if it is too big for just you, God has spoken.

Can you imagine walking with God and listening to his wisdom, to his heart for his people? To that, I say, "Stop imagining it, and start doing it!" Yes, God still speaks. We must still listen.

Noah and his family were saved, because he listened closely to God and then followed through with action. We, as new men, have washed away old sin. We have become new creatures in Christ Jesus. In baptism, we have "the pledge of good conscience toward God," and we, too, share in the resurrection of Jesus Christ!

3:22 who has gone into heaven and is at God's right hand—with angels, authorities and powers in submission to him.

When we submit our will, we say, "Lord, I am yours. Guide me, and direct me into all truth. I surrender my life to your leadership." Talk about freedom. The world says to hang on, to grab more power. Jesus says, "I am the way, the truth, and the life. Let go of the world, and let God fill you to overflowing." When we submit, we are in the company of angels, authority, and power. Not a bad place to be, right?

Peter ONE

Living for God

4:1 Therefore, since Christ suffered in his body, arm yourselves also with the same attitude, because whoever suffers in the body is done with sin.

Peter, are you telling us to have the same attitude as our Lord Jesus? Ok, yes, I see it. Since Jesus, who knew no sin, was beaten, bruised, and bloodied for our sin, we must see the power in arming ourselves in righteousness.

Romans 6:18: *"You have been set free from sin and have become slaves to righteousness."*

Can you remember the time when you did not know Christ? I have heard people say, "Well, I grew up in church. My family was always there. If the doors were open, we were there." Great. Some people had the opportunity at an early age to know of Christ. But did they know him? For us who lived the life of the un-churched, I can answer that question with a "yes." I can remember those times before I knew Christ as my Savior, the days when I had one purpose in mind: me! I did everything to satisfy my fleshly desires and to make me happy.

I can tell you that happiness was always three steps in front of me. I choose to remember what Christ has done

Peter ONE

for me. He came into my broken life and restored my relationship with Father God. He set me free.

The joy was three steps in front of me, and, when I took those steps, I realized that each step represented total surrender and restoration. The three steps are The Father, The Son, and The Holy Spirit. Restoration to God's heart, and a life restored. Yes, I can remember my life before I knew the Lord, but the light of his truth compels me forward, and the past becomes a very distant memory.

Peter says to "arm yourselves," and that's exactly what we must do. Put on the full armor of Christ. Put on the attitude of Christ. Suffering will produce a victory in Christ. When we are identified in his death (when we have accepted the work of the cross for us), we can also be identified in his life (following Christ in obedience and surrender). So, we arm ourselves in truth, and we make a stand to live our faith out loud. In other words, we don't hold back. Let's do this thing. In Christ, sin will lose its filthy hold on us. Life will be the real thing, amen?

4:2 As a result, they do not live the rest of their earthly lives for evil human desires, but rather for the will of God.

What results when we suffer in the body for having identified with the death, burial, and resurrection of our Lord Jesus, is that we are new creatures here on Earth. We realize what is to come is so much more than what has been. We live the rest of our earthly life to the

Peter ONE

fullest. We no longer strive to satisfy the flesh by running after or being comfortable with the sins that once were our friends.

We dispose of those like a sack full of garbage! Got that picture? You are done with that sin. You have thrown it out. So, why do so many of us fall for the temptation to dive headfirst into the dumpster of deceit to drag that sin back out? Sin disposed of, needs to stay in the dumpster. We need to consider cleaning up the rest of the trash in our lives, throwing out what we know is not of God and leaving it there in the dumpster. When we throw it out then try to retrieve it, we are wasting valuable time. We could be building a great life and creating a legacy here on Earth. Think about it.

I have seen people throw out their sin and then return the next day to jump into the dumpster to retrieve what they threw out! Nothing good can come out of that. You will be dirtier, smellier, and more contaminated. And you don't get dirty just from your old sin, but by everyone else's filthy sins, too. If you are in the dumpster at the wrong time, that big truck may pick you up, dump you into an even bigger mess, compress you to the point where you become one with the garbage, and then deposit you in a heap of rotten garbage with little chance of escape.

That is a picture of where I was, but I was rescued. I do not mean to sound disrespectful. In this analogy, God was a "trash picker," he picked me out of that mess, cleaned me up, ran me through his cleansing agent, and

Peter ONE

created something new. He created something better than my old self. So, if you are dealing with sinful garbage, don't delay. Throw it out, and then stay away from the dumpster.

We are to live the rest of our lives here on Earth for God. Seeking his will. Some of you have heard me say, "If you woke up this morning, and you are breathing, there is a purpose. That purpose is to glorify Father God."

4:3 For you have spent enough time in the past doing what pagans choose to do—living in debauchery, lust, drunkenness, orgies, carousing and detestable idolatry.

4:4 They are surprised that you do not join them in their reckless, wild living, and they heap abuse on you.

The cause and effect Peter writes about has not changed much over the generations. Remember, he encouraged us to live not in the flesh, but in the will of God. And here he says that enough is enough. In the past, we did what the world does in impurity and unrighteousness. When we choose the lust of the flesh, to get drunk, it is a choice. That might have been part of our lifestyle before we were followers of Christ. We may have taken part in debauchery. What does that mean? It must not happen anymore, because we never hear that word. Right? The word is a noun, meaning: "crazy

Peter ONE

partying and wild nights, usually accompanied by lots of alcohol" (vocabulary.com).

We may not hear the word much anymore, but we sure see the results of crazy parties and wild nights in our youth. Spring Break at Daytona Beach comes to mind. Maybe it should be called Spring Debauchery. If that were the case, kids would have a hard time convincing their parents to let them take the trip! Before you're yes and amen brother gets too loud, let me bring you back to the reality of those words.

Peter had seen the way of life of the pagans in that day, their seemingly never-ending search for satisfaction. Too much wine brings about drunkenness. When people lose their senses of right and wrong, then debauchery, lust, orgies, etc., follow. When one is delivered from the grasp of such living, the old friends and family who still live there cannot understand why you won't join in anymore.

Have you been in that situation? Or do you know someone who was tempted in that manner? I have, and it becomes a struggle of old vs. new. The party life or the straight and narrow? The world or the Kingdom of God?

We all have choices every day, and all around us are people trying to make good choices. Why do so many people attend AA meetings or Celebrate Recovery? Because they want to change, they just need help getting there.

Peter ONE

A good friend of mine leads Celebrate Recovery at a local church. Gary, my friend has such a heart for people, because he has been delivered from his past. If you are not familiar with Celebrate Recovery: it is a Biblical and balanced program that helps people overcome their hurts, hang-ups, and habits. With close to 20,000 churches worldwide participating, the chances are that you have heard of it. The encouraging thing to me is that so many people want to leave the lifestyle that has produced pain. They know that old life has left them broken, disgusted, disappointed, and disillusioned. They want to move out, move up, and move on. To do that, they need to get out of their old environments.

Not you? Good! Then help someone else have a victory over the old, and help them move on to a new life in Christ. Most of us shy away from stuff like that. We think someone else will do it, and maybe they will. The point is that if you pray about it and really seek the Lord's direction in how best to serve, he will show you how. For we who have been delivered and set free, the old life style was nothing more than a smokescreen. It had no substance, no future, no victory, no Father, no Son, and no Holy Spirit. It was just pain and disappointment.

So, when we see someone down and out, are we are we just thankful that isn't us anymore, or are we compelled to help? I hope we can see the benefit of helping. It is by the grace of God that we have been delivered, and we must walk in that grace. I recently heard someone say, "If you want to be better, you must

Peter ONE

be different." Jesus changes everything. When the world has you in a stranglehold and does not want to let you go, Jesus is the difference. He sets you free, and your old friends wonder why you won't "party on" with them anymore. But some will see the change in you and will want that for their own life. Some might even envy you for not waking up with a headache or hangover, and they might want to change.

If you want "better," be different. Of course, some of those so-called "friends" will want to "heap abuse on you," as Peter puts it. Remember, it is shame that causes people to do a lot of stupid things, and those stupid things drive shame even deeper. So, when they heap abuse on you, love them anyway.

4:5 But they will have to give account to him who is ready to judge the living and the dead.

Before you get self-righteous and say, "Good, they will get what they deserve," stop and think for a minute. Did you and I get what we deserved? No, we did not. We deserved death, but we were given a new life. Where you read that "they" will have to answer to God, keep in mind that we all do.

"The living and the dead" just about covers everyone, doesn't it? It covers people who are living today, actually walking around and breathing, and those who have gone on before. I was living and breathing on planet Earth, but I was dead in my sin until I accepted Jesus Christ as my Savior. That's when I went from death to

Peter ONE

life, and my heart was changed. I deserved nothing and received everything.

So, as we read in Romans 12:17: *"Do not repay anyone evil for evil. Be careful to do what is right in the eyes of everyone."* And, Romans 12:21: *"Do not be overcome by evil, but overcome evil with good."*

We have all sinned, and we all have fallen short of the mark. I want to walk in the freedom of Christ. I do not want to throw the first stone, nor the last. But if you and I would pray for those who try to drag us back into the crazy living that produces death, maybe they would come to know this crazy love found in Christ. They might join us in the hope of the future, this light that drives the darkness out!

4:6 For this is the reason the gospel was preached even to those who are now dead, so that they might be judged according to human standards in regard to the body, but live according to God in regard to the spirit.

What does Peter mean here? To preach the gospel to dead men? You are serious? Peter most likely was referring to the Gentiles. We must remember that the Jews regarded Gentiles as "spiritually dead," but Peter used this same word in the previous scripture, where "dead" meant, well, "dead", as in not breathing kind of dead.

Peter ONE

When I was dead in my sin, I was dead to the King of Kings. I was dead to my creator, in the sense that I knew not the beauty and wonder of the God of Abraham, Isaac, and Jacob. I was spiritually dead.

When I stop breathing on my last day on Earth, I will be considered clinically dead. So, when you think about Peter's statement, it doesn't need to be a point to ponder for weeks on end. Look at it this way: we all will be judged. We all have an eternity that we will spend in one of two places, those are Heaven or Hell. Your family and friends, also have a choice. The only gospel they may hear could be in your words. Choose them carefully, my friend. It may be a matter of life forever spent in freedom or death forever in the Lake of Fire.

Let our Father, through the power and grace of the Holy Spirit, give you the best words to speak, so that your "dead" friends and family may come to know Christ and be judged as living to the will, wonder, and word of our God. Only then can the dead know true life.

4:7 The end of all things is near. Therefore be alert and of sober mind so that you may pray.

Do you remember when people were predicting that the end is near, or when the Church was teaching on the rapture? There was a time when those messages were delivered from the pulpit, or from the street corner on a sandwich sign.

Peter ONE

I remember when, after a couple of sermons and some serious discussions at home, our daughter Aimee said, "Dad, I want to grow up and be a mommy, and I don't want the world to end." She has one of the sweetest hearts I know. For her, all of this talk of the world ending was producing worry and not peace. So with much reassurance, her mom and I did our best to make sure we focused on the presence of God, not the fire and brimstone. I am happy to report that she is a great wife and a "mommy" to two of the best boys you could ever meet. Oh, and her heart is still very sweet.

Needless to say, the world has not ended. Yet, when Peter wrote this, did he know that Jerusalem would be destroyed by the Romans? Did he know that the end of the Temple and Levitical priesthood, the end of the Jewish way of life, was here on Earth?

Good being bad, and bad being good, will end. *The Housewives of* Wherever... will end, as well as your favorite Bible teaching or TV network that you watch. All things will end, except the Kingdom of God has no end.

It has been said to every generation, "This could be it. Things are looking like God could wrap this all up." While that is true, the point is the second part of this verse: *"Be clear-minded and self-controlled so that you can pray."* Being clear-minded and self-controlled means having an uncluttered thought life so that we can actually think God thoughts. We need to be self-controlled and disciplined so that our life is a witness of God's grace in me.

Peter ONE

Then, there is the "prayer" thing. Yes, we are to seek God's direction through prayer. We are to listen when we pray – not just talk – and we are to pray constantly, in attitude and in word. Not "if you pray," but when we pray. There have been volumes written on prayer, the power of prayer, and the glorious reports of answered prayer. For me, prayer is a simple conversation with my Heavenly Father. He knows when I mess up, and he knows what I need more than I do.

He loves us, cares for us, wants the very best for us, and likes to hear from us. When our minds are clear and our lives under control, those conversations are not out of fear, but delivered out of faith.

Yes, the end may very well be close, but, until it arrives, we are to live each day in a spirit of gratitude. A spirit of love reaches those who need to hear the good news of Jesus Christ.

4:8 Above all, love each other deeply, because love covers over a multitude of sins.

It seems like I have heard that before. James finishes his letter with this same thought. Here is James 5:20: *"Remember this, whoever turns a sinner from the error of his way will save him from death and cover over a multitude of sins."*

Now Peter reveals how to turn a sinner from his way, how to save him from death. He says to, above all, love each other deeply. Love is and has always been the

Peter ONE

answer. God is love, we are his, and we are instruments of love. *"God so loved the world that he gave his one and only Son, that whoever believes in him shall not perish but have eternal life"* (John 3:16 NIV).

The Bee-Gee's had that song entitled "How Deep is your Love." It is a great question. Of course, we need the deep, abiding love of the heart of God. Great love songs are good, and they have a place, but deep, abiding love can be traced back to the source.

1 John 4:10 reads: *"This is love: not that we loved God, but that he loved us and sent his Son as an atoning sacrifice for our sins."*

He loves you. He made you. He wants the very best for you. Got it? I certainly hope so. He first loved us, and he created us with the capacity to love him and others deeply. So, if no one has asked recently, I will. How deep is your love? We love our family deeply, but what about a stranger? We care about the people we love, and that is why love covers a multitude of sins. Our love cannot remove the sin from another life. Only the Blood of Jesus can do that.

Because you love deeply, you are kind and gentle in conduct toward others. Love has a way of overlooking faults, of not being so judgmental. It helps us give charity to those whose imperfections would normally drive us crazy. I'm sure you have heard "Love is blind." What that means is that, yes, you may still do things that drive me crazy, but I don't notice them as much. When

Peter ONE

you love someone, it's as if they can do no wrong in your eyes. So, our love will cover over a multitude of sin, but not remove them. Our love will show the world that Christ is in us, the Hope of Glory.

Jesus sums this up in John 13:34-35: *"A new command I give you: Love one another. As I have loved you, so you must love one another. By this everyone will know that you are my disciples, if you love one another."*

We love, because he made us to love. He showed us how to love and how to operate in love. Can you imagine for a moment what this planet would be like if we all loved deeply? It would kind of be like Heaven, I think.

4:9 Offer hospitality to one another without grumbling.

Be ready to offer what you have to one another. Be ready to break bread and divide it with the hungry. Give what you have to those who have not. It is not always easy. Many saints in the Church have the gift of hospitality. They know how to make people feel welcome and loved, and they do it so well.

"Can't I leave this kind of stuff to them? Can't I just push people in their direction?" Sure, you can, and you can also miss a great reward that was meant for you. We are all called to love. We are all called to treat everyone with dignity and respect. We are all called to share our material blessings with those in need.

Peter ONE

My wife would give everything we have to those in need. She is a generous, loving woman of God, and I admire that so much. I, on the other hand, have to work hard at hospitality. Over the years, I have gotten better, but I still have a long way to go. Oh, I give, but it isn't always without grumbling. If only I could be more generous!

I have examined why I struggle in that area, and I think I may have discovered why. Growing up, my family had few material possessions. When we did get something, it seemed like it never lasted. Moving around so much, from state to state, we never accumulated anything of value. Or so I thought. True enough, we never had much, but we had each other. We knew we were loved. Knowing that is of great value. As an adult, when I actually accumulated, I wanted to hold on too tightly. I am learning and getting better, and, evidently, God is not done with me yet.

4:10 Each of you should use whatever gift you have received to serve others, as faithful stewards of God's grace in its various forms.

What is your gift or talent? Whatever it is, you have been given it for a purpose, and that purpose is to serve others. By serving others, you are a reflection of God's love. How do you recognize your gift? Well, there are several good programs, tests, and evaluations one can take, but here is a short process you may want to consider.

Peter ONE

1. Pray: Pray that God the Father reveals your "specific" gift to your heart and mind.

2. Listen: Prayer works best when we listen more than we talk. So, listen to that still, small voice.

3. Pray some more: Pray for clarity on what you hear when you listen.

4. Notice: Start to notice what makes you excited in the Kingdom. The chances are that God put that excitement in you for a reason.

5. Do: After you have prayed, listened, prayed some more, and noticed, step out in faith. Do whatever God is leading you to do, wherever he is leading you to do it.

Fear holds too many believers back. It is time to put your talents to work. Give your gift! The Kingdom will be better. The lives you touch, the people you bless, and you yourself will be much better off as a result.

The Word of God speaks of many of these gifts, but here are just a few: Administration, Apostle, Celibacy, Artist, Encouragement, Evangelist, Exhortation, Faith, Giving, Healing, Hospitality, Prayer, Leadership, Mercy, Miracles, Missionary, Music Pastor, Teacher, Wisdom, Writing. Whew! Isn't it good to know that you don't have to have all of these? I have met some people who seem to have them all, but remember that, right now, the focus is on you.

Peter ONE

4:11 If anyone speaks, they should do so as one who speaks the very words of God. If anyone serves, they should do so with the strength God provides, so that in all things God may be praised through Jesus Christ. To him be the glory and the power for ever and ever. Amen.

The "anyone" here is targeted at preachers, or the offices of ministry. In other words, if you are a speaker, speak the words of the Lord. Of course, any of us can speak the Word of God, and we should. To speak wisely, use the Word to speak love. Speak the Word to edify your friends, family, and neighbors. The Word of God is a great way to do it. Have you ever been around people who just want to speak so that they can hear themselves? They have a desire to fill the air with whatever flows from the recesses of their minds. They would much rather babble with BS than speak truth from God's Word.

It is an awesome responsibility – a privilege – to stand before a group, class, or congregation to speak. But all of us are given opportunity to glorify God by the words that we allow to come from our mouth. The objective is to speak God's truth. If you are going to do that, you first must know the truth and the Word of truth. Know God and his truth that sets men free.

The truth in us compels truth to come out of us. Reading and studying the Word of God, allowing the penetrating truth to soak deep into your heart, doesn't just change the way you think. It changes the way you speak.

Peter ONE

When you speak and serve, do it with the strength of God. In other words, serve in the ability that he has given you. When I learned this, I was set free. It had always been about me. That was the old, selfish me. God had given me the desire to teach, and he had allowed me the opportunity to speak. I spoke about good, about success, and about getting ahead. It was all good, but it was not great.

Through the years, I have come to see that it is not about me. If God allows my voice to be heard, I want it to be his words that come out of my mouth. If my feet carry me to a place – near or far – I want it to be for the glory of a living and loving God.

If I am called to serve, I want to serve from a heart filled with gratitude and thankfulness, so that, in all things, God may be praised through Jesus Christ.

"To him be the glory and the power forever and ever, amen."

Peter could have ended his letter right there. I mean, he said, "Amen," right? The scriptures from 1 Peter 4:1-11 are given the subtitle "Living for God." Peter could have said his final, "Amen," on the subject, but he wanted to make sure that readers understood we are to live for God. There will be challenges and suffering along the way!

Peter ONE

Suffering for Being a Christian

4:12 Dear friends, do not be surprised at the fiery ordeal that has come on you to test you, as though something strange were happening to you.

Do not be surprised. When we walk in the name of Jesus, in integrity and truth, painful things still happen. Why shouldn't we be surprised? When Peter wrote this, tragic things were happening in the early church. If you called yourself a Christian and followed the Way, your life was open for persecution.

It was a common occurrence, so Peter wrote to not be surprised. Don't think it strange. Your faith will be tested. It will be put through the fire. He also pleaded with the believers to exhort one another to face the testing of one's faith with patience and integrity.

Friend, the Church has seen these painful trials and sufferings over the centuries. It is most obvious in the early church, and then came some great years of growth during the revivals. During the Reformation time period, the laws of the land were a reflection of the Laws of God.

But if history is a good teacher, we are headed to more and more persecution as a Church. Many have said, "The only thing necessary for the triumph of evil is for good men to do nothing."

Peter ONE

I fear that many good men have done nothing and that evil is gaining ground. Look around. It seems that the world has gone mad. The influence of the Church is the only thread holding society together. In a day where there is no right or wrong, how can we be surprised that pain and suffering are so evident? Please, do not be one of those good men who do nothing. Stand up for your faith. In the name of Jesus, take a stand for what's right. "If you don't stand for something, you'll fall for anything."

2 Chronicles 20:17: *"Take up your positions, stand firm and see the deliverance the Lord will give you. Do not be afraid, do not be discouraged. Go out and face them tomorrow, and the Lord will be with you."*

Luke 21:28: *"When these things begin to take place, stand up and lift up your heads, because your redemption is drawing near."*

So, don't be surprised when your faith is tested. Don't lose heart, but know that this testing will produce purity and strength. Our enemy, the devil, is defeated when he throws everything he has at a follower of Christ, and the outcome produces a deep abiding faith in Gods people. Oh, he can't stand it! So, don't be surprised. It is not strange that this cosmic battle is fought at the heart level!

4:13 But rejoice inasmuch as you participate in the sufferings of Christ, so that you may be overjoyed when his glory is revealed.

Peter ONE

Rejoice in suffering? I don't know many people who want to hear that. When someone is in the midst of pain and suffering, the last thing they want to hear is, "Rejoice." The comforting power of our living God is what makes suffering endurable. When we suffer in Christ for the Kingdom, his grace and mercy cover us, and they allow us to know that this suffering is not in vain. It produces a measure of glory. When our mind set is on him and our heart one with him, his suffering becomes ours, and our sufferings for Christ are his. The glory that is produced far outweighs the pain of the suffering. Rejoice, yes, that you can be "one" in Christ Jesus. He loves you that much! So much that he would allow you to suffer for his sake, as he suffered for yours, is truly amazing love.

Then, when victory is produced, we become overwhelmed by his love, overjoyed in his presence, and overcome completely by his glory. I truly feel for people who choose to face adversity alone. Without Christ, it is all magnified intensity. To think of one facing it all alone is almost unbearable. Yet, I remember those days of trying to figure it out myself, and it makes my relationship with Christ so much the sweeter. Rejoice, and let his glory be revealed!

4:14 If you are insulted because of the name of Christ, you are blessed, for the Spirit of glory and of God rests on you.

People might make fun of your decision to give your life to Jesus. Christians have been called all sorts of names

Peter ONE

down through the years. Trust me; it is not fun when it happens to you! People who try to operate with the veil covering their faces and dulling their minds will attack a peaceful mind and loving faith, because they feel threatened. Many people fear what they do not understand.

Read 2 Corinthians 3:12-18. Think on it. We, too, were veiled. We had no idea that the truth could be so freedom-filled. We found that out in verse 16. *"But whenever anyone turns to the Lord, the veil is taken away."* How can we condemn people who have not yet had the veil removed? We can't. It is not our job to condemn anyone. Only God almighty can do that. I certainly do not want the responsibility that comes with that. I am not qualified to sit in judgment, and neither are you.

Our "job" then, as believers, is to love even those people who hate us. Love as Christ loves. Plant the seeds, and pray for the harvest. Remember that God's Word is true. Peter is saying that we are blessed if we are insulted for the name of Christ. Because we are his, then we are B-L-E-S-S-E-D. I know it doesn't always feel like it, but truth is truth. Over the years, I have been considered a "fuddy-duddy." Most recently, I was called "out of touch." This is because I was taught right from wrong when I was growing up, and I still believe it.

The Word of God is plain and simple, until it starts stepping on our own toes. We can read what's right for everyone else, but when we read, and when the Holy

Peter ONE

Spirit convicts us and reveals truth to our hearts, we must repent and give it to God.

If being out of touch means that I cannot sit and watch the housewives of wherever tearing someone down, or that I can't watch a cooking show in which they have to "bleep" out every other word, then call me "out of touch." I really don't mind. My goal is not to be in touch with a world that demeans my faith, but to be in touch with my Savior, the creator of the universe, and the true Judge. This allows you and I to reach the world for Christ. I want the veil removed, and I do not want a fuzzy faith. The truth needs to be bold and clear in our lives.

"And we, who with unveiled faces all reflect the Lord's glory are being transformed into his likeness with ever-increasing glory which comes from the Lord, who is the Spirit" (2 Corinthians 3:18).

Our call as Christians is the great commission:

"Then Jesus came to them and said, 'All authority in heaven and on earth has been given to me. Therefore go and make disciples of all nations, baptizing them in the name of the Father and of the Son and of the Holy Spirit'" (Matthew 28:18-19).

Nowhere does it say that you will not have trouble. I don't see anywhere where the Bible says it will be easy. We are told we will have trouble, that there will be opposition, and that we may be insulted because we believe in Christ. We are surely blessed to be called his

Peter ONE

followers when the Spirit of Glory and the Glory of God rest on us. The world will attack, and insults will be thrown like stones.

Rejoice! Again, I say rejoice! You bear the image of a mighty God who loves you and who will never leave you. Walk in the assurance of the faith, in the power of the Holy Spirit, and in the grace and mercy that come only from the love of Christ. You are his, and he is yours.

4:15 If you suffer, it should not be as a murderer or thief or any other kind of criminal, or even as a meddler.

Have you ever brought about pain and suffering on yourself? Of course you have. We all have. Many times, this comes about by our acting before we think it through.

Paul uses some examples of self-induced suffering, so let's explore this closer. Murder? Of course you would suffer. Look in Exodus 2:11-15. Moses saw an Egyptian beating a Hebrew. The scripture says Moses "glanced this way and that," in order to make sure no one was around. He killed the Egyptian and hid him in the sand. Moses committed murder, and he ran. It changed his entire life. He suffered, but he was still used by God.

In Acts 5:1-11, we read of a man and his wife who stole the glory and lied to the Holy Spirit. The deception cost them their very lives. The crime? Dishonest behavior

Peter ONE

before God. Let's just say that they never did it again. Aren't you glad that we operate under grace and mercy? I am! So, if we suffer, it should not be as men who lie, cheat, steal, murder, or meddle!

4:16 However, if you suffer as a Christian, do not be ashamed, but praise God that you bear that name.

Right now, somewhere a Christian is being threatened, imprisoned, persecuted, or beheaded for their faith.

In the Western Church, we know little of the magnitude of their suffering. Oh, we would like to think that we are suffering, and there are times when I certainly do not understand why things happen to the Church and God's people. But, for the most part, we have freedom to worship and freedom to fulfill the great commission.

If we suffer because of the name of Christ, for being called a Christian, we can praise God that we bear that name. We must not be ashamed of the gospel, and, if we refuse to suffer or to account for it, are we just giving lip service to the true faith?

If we are despised or mistreated, and we will be if we are serving Our God, keep in mind , all Christ our Savior did for us. He was an innocent man in whom no fault was found. But, he was beaten and bruised for our transgressions. He was displayed in public, yet he held his tongue. He was nailed to a cross and died a humiliating death. Why? He did this for you and I, for our

Peter ONE

children and grandchildren, and for generations to come. He took our shame so that we could be free. We are free to stand up and to not deny the faith. We are free to live a life in pursuit of righteousness. We have freedom to choose this day whom we will serve. We must wear the "Christian" name well and without shame when the media decides to bash Christians or when the latest TV or movie portrays Christians as weird or fanatical.

Here is the challenge: step up. You are a child of the living God, but you are not a baby. Stand up, step up, and rise up in the name of Jesus. Seldom do we see open persecution. Persecution is now on the rise in a more subtle way.

The faith has been watered down and diluted for a few generations, so its power is diminished. God's power is as strong as ever, but we, his people, are not. If you call yourself a Christian, then act like it. Quit flirting with the things of this world. Quit trying to live a small faith. You living small does this dying world no good. Live out loud, stand for what's right, pray hard, and seek justice.

Sure, you may experience reproach and scorn, just like Jesus did. But is that a good reason to not walk your faith out? The world hates a Christian who confesses Jesus as Savior and then lives it out. If you are going to be ashamed, then be ashamed of what is wrong. Glory in what is right, regardless of the consequences to you.

Peter ONE

Last time I checked, it is still against the law to burn Christians at the stake! Yes, there are those who verbally assault believers for the faith. Our response should be to pray that the living, loving God be revealed. But we cannot hide in fear I have seen friends and family disown fellow believers, just because they confess Jesus as Lord. Friends who feel threatened by a true faith will cease to be friends. It takes away their excuses when one of their friends escapes an ungodly lifestyle and finds freedom. This is the same spirit that the early Church experienced, and what was their response? They did not stop spreading the Way. They did not give up, but, in power, they moved the Kingdom forward. They were not ashamed of Christ. In the face of opposition, we must take this same stance. Let God be glorified, and praise him who counts us worthy to suffer for his name.

Let others see our true convictions, and be thankful we are called "Christians."When we stand up in love, the world will take note. When the world takes note, they may see what truth looks like. When they see truth, they may want what we have. Does it make sense?

STAND UP, STEP OUT, AND GIVE GOD THE GLORY. In the victory and in the suffering, regardless of the outcome, give God glory. When we do this either out of joy or pain and suffering it places the praise where it belongs on our Father who loves us.

4:17 For it is time for judgment to begin with God's household; and if it begins with us, what

Peter ONE

will the outcome be for those who do not obey the gospel of God?

Do you find it consoling that judgment starts with us believers, with the family of God? We all pass under the judgment of the Creator. The judgment has already begun, but on the "day of judgment," all will stand before God. Today, when you read the Word of God, the "two-edged sword," does not the judgment cut both ways? In other words, it saves some and condemns others.

We read in Hebrews 4:12: *"For the Word of God is alive and active. Sharper than any double-edged sword it penetrates even to dividing soul and spirit, joints and marrow; it judges the thoughts and attitudes of the heart."*

We, the family of God, are always being judged by the power of the Word. This Word goes right to the heart, and it cuts through the confusion, the mess, and the nonsense of this world. Nothing – absolutely nothing – is hidden from God's sight. He sees, he knows, he is ever present, and he is all knowing. So, if judgment has started, and is ongoing, why not begin with his family?

He is just and holy. I, for one, would much rather face his judgment than the judgment of some on Earth who have appointed themselves judge and jury. They do not know my heart, my thoughts, or my actions and deeds. When I face my maker, I can and do claim the Blood of Jesus over my sin.

Peter ONE

When Peter asks, "What will the outcome be for who do not obey the gospel of God?" he has positioned it correctly. If we who are in Christ Jesus are rightly judged by the Word, and by God, then how bad will it be for those who are not in Christ?

You and I know people who will face the judgment, people who will be condemned if they do not discover Jesus and his mercy personally. The question is: how do we reach them with the Gospel, the Good News of the Kingdom? We grab on to the Great Commission and do all we know and are called to do in Matthew 28:18-20: "Go, and make Disciples." If we do not, we face judgment for knowing and not doing. Here is a hard question; Do you have the boldness and tenacity to share the good news? Some will say, "hey that is the preachers job, that responsibility belongs to the church". To which I say, "hello…we are the church".

The people we do not reach face the eternal judgment of rejecting Jesus Christ. We have an awesome responsibility – we must move the Kingdom forward.

4:18 And, "If it is hard for the righteous to be saved, what will become of the ungodly and the sinner?"

I was sitting with a group of men recently, and the subject of "doing it ourselves" came up. A couple of things came out of this conversation that I need to share with you. First, we have no power apart from Christ in us. We need to approach our Father with childlike faith.

Peter ONE

We are not worms saved by grace. We are new creatures, made new by the Power of God. The old is dead, and we need to bury that person once and for all.

If it is hard for believers to accept what the Lord Jesus has done to save them, how can the ungodly be saved? I take this as a personal assignment – to walk in a childlike faith that is always growing in righteousness. I want to keep it simple enough that anyone can see it can be done. Total surrender to our Great God, through the saving blood of Jesus, brings us into salvation.

Why do we make it hard by adding our own "Rules and Regulations" of Christian living? We can do nothing without the Life of God in us. Accept this life Jesus has called you to and then grow in your faith. Does it sound doable? It is.

4:19 So then, those who suffer according to God's will should commit themselves to their faithful Creator and continue to do good.

Peter is telling us to stay the course. Suffering for the Kingdom is no reason to quit. You and I were born into a world at war. The cosmic battle between the forces of evil and the absolute good of God has been raging since the fall of man. Keep in mind that this world is not our home. Oh, we become very comfortable in our routines, but if we don't suffer setbacks, the chances are that we are not attempting great things for God. If we remain safe and ineffective, we may suffer less, but we may never know the taste of great victories for God.

Peter ONE

Because we wanted to play it safe, we might miss a friend's decision to follow Christ, because we never planted a seed. We might not catch a glimpse of our children and grandchildren returning to the faith, because of our lack of faithfulness. I do not have any idea of what suffering you are going through right now, but you are GOING THROUGH it, amen? Keep going. Our Faithful God honors his faithful followers.

When you read something like, "Suffer according to God's will," what do you think? Suffering? I don't want that! Well, no one likes to suffer, unless they know that the outcome is worth it. Yes, God will allow you to suffer. He will use this to build character, strengthen resolve, and deepen your faith. For this, we need to be thankful and commit ourselves to our faithful Creator. Continue to do good. Continue to glorify Father God in all you do.

He made us, he designed a life to be lived forever, and he has given us all that we need to do good. If we have received the gift of Jesus and his work on the cross, our gift in return is to commit ourselves to the faithful Creator, to live this life to honor our faithful Creator.

To Elders and Young Men

5:1 To the elders among you, I appeal as a fellow elder and a witness of Christ's sufferings who also will share in the glory to be revealed

Peter ONE

Peter is most likely not talking to the "old" among his readers, though most elders and officers of the church were older in years. If you reached this point in life, you must have some wisdom about you. Yeah, you would think so.

Peter is saying, "Look, I am an elder too, and I saw firsthand how Jesus suffered." Yes, he did. In the Gospels we see how Peter was called by the Son of God to follow him. He was a fisherman, and that's how Jesus called him: "Come, I will make you fishers of men."

Jesus called Peter (known as Simon, remember the name change), and Peter's brother, Andrew. They both were fishermen. Then, he called James and John, the sons of Zebedee. They were fishermen, too. Jesus is still calling men today – reaching people right where they are. He said to a fisherman, "Come, I will let you fish for men's souls and spirits." To the welder, he may be saying, "Come I will let you weld families back together." To the electrician, maybe it's, "Come, you will share the light of the world." To the chef, perhaps, "Come, follow me, and I will let you feed the world with my words of truth."

Jesus still is calling. To the salesperson, he may be saying, "Come, I will let you promote the Kingdom. Sell out to me, and your life will change forever." Jesus calls to the teachers, "Come, follow me. Learn from me, and I will let you teach and reach children for the future."

Peter ONE

Can you see it? Jesus calls to the stockbroker, "Come, follow me, and I will help you trade your old life for the future good." Regardless of our station in life, the Lord is calling us to follow him. Peter happened to be a fisherman, and when he was called he left his nets and followed Jesus.

When you were called, did you leave anything behind? I did. I left a life of shame, misery, and disappointment. I left my "net" of discouragement and despair, and I found a life worth living. "Come, and I will make you a fisher of men." I did, and he did.

Remember, Peter saw firsthand the sufferings of Christ. He saw him arrested in the Garden at the Mount of Olives. He remembered what Jesus had said about, "Before the rooster crows today, you will deny three times that you know me" (Luke 22:34). Peter did deny Christ, and he ended up outside weeping bitterly.

Oh, the pain. But when Peter writes the second part of First Peter 5:1, we see the hope: "And one who also will share in the glory to be revealed." This Peter who denied Jesus was reinstated after Jesus rose from the dead, just as he said he would do. I know we have looked at this earlier, but it may be worth another look, re-read this great story of power, glory, and redemption in John chapters 20-21:

"15 When they had finished eating, Jesus said to Simon Peter, 'Simon son of John, do you love me more than these?'

Peter ONE

'Yes, Lord,' he said, 'you know that I love you.'

Jesus said, 'Feed my lambs.'

[16] Again Jesus said, 'Simon son of John, do you love me?'

He answered, 'Yes, Lord, you know that I love you.'

Jesus said, 'Take care of my sheep.'

[17] The third time he said to him, 'Simon son of John, do you love me?'

Peter was hurt, because Jesus asked him the third time, "Do you love me?" He said, "Lord, you know all things; you know that I love you."

Jesus said, "Feed my sheep."

When Peter says that he saw firsthand the suffering of Jesus, he meant it. He also suffered the shame and humiliation of the denial of a friend. He was then given a Kingdom assignment to feed the Lord's sheep. Three times he denied Jesus, and three times he had to verify his love for the Lord, by consenting to do the Lords will, a unique repentance, indeed.

But here is the point: when you feel like you have messed up and can never come back to the Lord, that is a lie. He is always waiting for us, asking, "Do you love

Peter ONE

me?" How we answer that question is critical. For Peter, it set the stage for the rest of his life.

He became a shepherd, feeding the Lord's sheep. He went from fisherman, to follower, to denier, and to shepherd. What a journey! Then, he challenges us with the same challenge that Jesus gave him.

5:2 Be shepherds of God's flock that is under your care, watching over them—not because you must, but because you are willing, as God wants you to be; not pursuing dishonest gain, but eager to serve;

5:3 not lording it over those entrusted to you, but being examples to the flock.

"Do you love me?" asks Jesus. "Then feed my sheep." Be shepherds, overseers, elders, brothers, and sisters. Love each other as Christ loves you. Forgive one another, and show mercy and grace to the flock. Let the world see whose you are.

If you are in a leadership role in the Church today, you need to ask, "Why?" Why am I leading this flock? Why am I involved with this ministry? The answer is (check one):

1. I need this job. I have bills to pay. _____

2. I need to serve. God called me here. _____

Peter ONE

Ok. Now that you have been honest with yourself, listen again to what Peter says: "Not because you must, but because you are willing, as God wants you to be; not greedy for money, but eager to serve."

So maybe the question really is: are you willing to serve as God calls? Recently, a friend of mine's son, who is on staff at a church in Dallas, had been presented with the opportunity to move his family to either New York or Washington state. One ministry was a church plant, and the other was an established church, complete with people! One was to build, and the other came fully assembled. Either meant moving family out of the comfort zone, either choice meant going and serving. The choice they made was made through prayer and leading of the Holy Spirit. Which one did they choose? Well let's just say, I hope they like the mountains.

Whatever you are doing for God, do it boldly. Step out, and trust him to equip you. Do all things as unto the Lord, and, if you are in leadership, remember that you are being led by the Holy Spirit of God. If you are not following God, why would you expect anyone to follow your lead? Peter says not to lord it over those entrusted to you, but to be an example to the flock. Does that mean anything to you?

I have seen pastors and priests who think they are better than the people they are serving. With Christ as our example, I do not see that attitude in his ministry. He did not tell Pilate at the trumped up trial of all time, "Look, buddy, don't you know who I am?" He did exactly

Peter ONE

what Father had told him. May I suggest we do the same? Leadership in a local or global organization does not give you the right to think you're better than the "least of these" that you are serving. Pray for clear direction, and let God be God. Let him lead your heart, your mind, and your hands. A change may be in order! Many times he will give us more than one option, like my friends son, and he leaves the choice up to us. Choose wisely through prayer, Amen?

5:4 And when the Chief Shepherd appears, you will receive the crown of glory that will never fade away.

If you are in leadership, know that you were placed there for a purpose. That purpose is to glorify the loving Lord, not to bring self glory. In humility, be heavenly minded as you serve. If we can reach one more life with the saving message of Jesus Christ, the chief shepherd is pleased. If we preach a watered-down gospel, build a bigger parking lot, or have a great worship band, some people are happy.

Don't get me wrong. I know that the programs and ministries in the Church are good. But if they are not bringing people to Christ, we may be missing the point. Preacher, feed my sheep. Pastor, care for the flock. Teacher, feed my lambs. Do not take lightly the Kingdom assignment that you have been given, and let's together reach one more life for Christ.

Peter ONE

When the Chief Shepherd, Jesus himself, appears to see what you have done with your call, he will judge the work and your heart. Were you just doing a job for a wage, or did you pour your life into the flock? Your reward will be a crown of glory that will never fade away.

5:5 In the same way, you who are younger, submit yourselves to your elders. All of you, clothe yourselves with humility toward one another, because,

> "God opposes the proud
> but shows favor to the humble."

"Young men." Just what is Peter talking about here? How young? Think about it. Do you know anyone younger than you? Of course you do. What about older than you? Sure. Then that qualifies you to follow Peter's direction. If you're young, realize that the men who have gone before you have paved the way. They might just know a thing or two about life and Kingdom service.

We are encouraged to clothe ourselves with humility for a reason. During the time Peter wrote this letter, there was a garment that was worn by slaves and servants that resembled a long, white apron. It was an outer garment that made it clear that this was a person serving in a specific capacity.

 Speaking of aprons, growing up, it seemed my mom worked all the time. In the early years, she was a waitress. Back then, her uniform was either black with a

Peter ONE

white apron, or it was white with a black apron. She had a little hat that was similar to a nurse's. She looked the part of a professional, because she was.

For most Americans, going out to eat was a big deal. We did it once a month, or once a week, maybe. The person who was handling your food and giving you service needed to look like they knew what they were doing. Those tips that Mom earned by giving great service became milk money for six kids. Did she wear those garments because she wanted to? Or did she wear them because it was required? Actually it was both. My Mom was the best, and she always looked the best. She came to serve people every day, and, as a result, the bills got paid. She put on the garment of service. She humbled herself for her family, and she served others with a smile and a grateful heart.

Can we say that? Are we serving God and others with a glad heart? We must humble ourselves. We must put on the garment of service, and we must do our best to remain humble. Are we willing to take any place, to perform any task that God calls us to? Are we willing to do all things as unto the Lord? I certainly hope so. When we allow pride to raise its ugly head, we risk losing humility. Let me give you an example of a Christian follower who chose humility.

In the early Church, many followers of Christ actually sold themselves into slavery, in order that they might take the good news to people who were in bondage. Think of that: someone who is willing to humble themselves for the good of the Kingdom of God. They were willing to take on the garment of service that would become a garment of praise. Who would be willing to give up everything to be a servant?

One such person comes to mind.

Mother Teresa, the Blessed Teresa of Calcutta, is the person that comes to my mind. She left a comfortable life at the convent to step out in faith to care for the "poorest among the poor." She referred to it as "the call within the call." The Sisters of Charity and the Missionaries of Charity operate hospices, family counseling, orphanages, and schools. They number more than 4,500 sisters. They are active in over 130 countries. They exist, because this little nun chose to humble herself to serve a mighty God. She won a Nobel Peace Prize and many other awards, including the Presidential Medal of Freedom from Ronald Regan in 1985.

Mother Teresa once said, "By blood, I am Albanian; by citizenship, an Indian; by faith, I am a Catholic Nun. As to my calling, I belong to the world. As to my heart, I belong entirely to the heart of Jesus."

If you ever get the chance to see the documentary "*Something Beautiful for God*," or if you can ever read the book of the same title, I would highly recommend it. We may not be a Mother Teresa, but we do belong to the heart of Christ. We are his, and we need to humble ourselves before God and put on the garment of service.

Peter ONE

Who of us would dare say, "Here I am, send me?" Who would be willing to go anywhere, to do anything for our Lord? You and I may never be called to India or Africa, but we may be called across town, or to right next door. Remember, God opposes the proud, but he gives grace to the humble. I, for one, do not want to be opposed by God!

Please pray the following with me:

"Oh Lord, forgive me of my pride and my unwillingness to be used for your purpose. Please let me see clearly your call. Give me grace for the journey, and let me experience your love and mercy as I seek first your will and your Kingdom. Grow my faith to match your call, in Jesus Name. Amen."

5:6 Humble yourselves, therefore, under God's mighty hand, that he may lift you up in due time.

Why do many Christian leaders struggle with being humble in circumstance and humble in spirit? I think I have some insight into that. Any man or woman in leadership is just that – man or woman. We are all human people, regardless of the call. I find it very interesting that the flock that is made up of people expects perfection from the Pastor, the Worship Leader, the Elders, the Staff, or even the church parking lot Traffic Director. But we give little thought to the imperfections in our own life! If we can all get to the point of self-examination – if we can all work on

Peter ONE

ourselves and humble ourselves – the rest of the world has fewer problems.

Peter encourages us to "humble ourselves." I once heard someone say, "I think I would much rather humble myself than have God humble me." I agree. I must humble myself.

What is "humble?" The definition is, "Marked by meekness or modesty in behavior, attitude, or spirit; not arrogant or prideful." So, if we are to humble ourselves, we must be willing to take a low place. We have to be meek (not weak) in spirit, and we have to destroy pride and haughtiness in our actions. We then can operate under the Mighty Hand of God. Imagine that! You humble yourself under the direction of the Creator of the universe, and he sees that heart of service. He sees that you are subjected to him. Then, he will, in due time, lift you up. The "due time" is his perfect time – his proper time to accomplish his will. When we humble ourselves, we get to play a part in the great story of salvation.

Most people want it now! Not in due time, but now! And our loving Father smiles and says, "Oh, child, I love you enough to change you from the inside out." So, we wait. In the perfect, proper time, we are lifted up for his glory.

5:7 Cast all your anxiety on him because he cares for you.

Why don't we get this? We have a Father who not only knows best, but who knows everything. He is not

Peter ONE

surprised when we feel like we can't handle one more thing. He cares so much for you that he made a way of escaping eternal death, and he made a way through Christ to eternal life

Someone said, "Hey, if bad things are happening to you, don't worry. God signed off on it." I guess that's true, in a sense. Just as he did with Job, and just as he did with all the Apostles – including Peter – during their lifetimes, God allows suffering. God wants to show his grace and mercy through his care and love for you. He is the Almighty and he is Sovereign! There is no better place to cast our burdens, anxieties, and problems.

Some would rather suffer "out loud" than to trust God. Let me explain. If you take your problems to your family, friends, co-workers, and everyone who will lend a compassionate ear, it really may help for a moment. But it resolves little. As a matter of fact, it could affect your relationships. If all people hear from you is your issues, fears, and complaining, relationships suffer.

Why not try what Peter is encouraging us to do? Cast your cares on God. Know that he is bigger, much bigger, than any problem. Leave the issue in his capable, powerful, and loving hands. You will walk in freedom, and you will be much more effective than if you carry the burden around, trying to dump it on everyone else. Amen?

Peter goes on to instruct us on how to stand firm in utmost character and strength.

Peter ONE

5:8 Be alert and of sober mind. Your enemy the devil prowls around like a roaring lion looking for someone to devour.

Some translations start this passage with, "Be sober." It is not addressing drinking, it means to be serious. Being self-controlled and alert, for some people, is like spitting into the wind. It doesn't work so well.

Read from The Message:

8-11 Keep a cool head. Stay alert. The Devil is poised to pounce, and would like nothing better than to catch you napping. Keep your guard up. You're not the only ones plunged into these hard times. It's the same with Christians all over the world. So keep a firm grip on the faith. The suffering won't last forever. It won't be long before this generous God who has great plans for us in Christ—eternal and glorious plans they are!—will have you put together and on your feet for good. He gets the last word; yes, he does.

The point is that we need to be centered in Christ, having our flesh under submission and authority. We need to be wide-awake. We must be vigilant to the truth. Because, when we are, we recognize the lies of our enemy, Satan. His job is to kill, steal, and destroy. If you belong to Christ, yes, he is your enemy. Satan has been waging war against man since the beginning with his

Peter ONE

deceptions. He has come as a subtle serpent, an angel of light, and a roaring lion. As humans living temporarily in this fallen world, we must be aware that we do have an enemy. The battle is real, and we need to be alert. With eyes wide open, be ready for battle!

This "roaring lion" makes every effort to create fear in his prey. Consider this: if you are not prayed up, you will be preyed upon. If you are not strong in the spirit, you become weak in the flesh. If you do not walk by faith, you will operate out of fear. So, when you hear the loud roar of the lion, fear makes you an easy target.

Lions roar the loudest when they are hungry, and they become fierce when they seek their next meal. You don't want to become that! You don't want to be a meal, or even a snack, for the enemy. When you hear the roar of the lion, you need to be strong enough to know that it's really a lie. So how do we stand against this enemy in strength and faith? I'm glad you asked.

5:9 Resist him, standing firm in the faith, because you know that the family of believers throughout the world is undergoing the same kind of suffering.

    See that?   R-E-S-I-S-T

                  Rely on God

                  Every Day

Peter ONE

Seek him first

In all things

Stay strong and

Trust the Lord

RESIST

Satan cannot devour us when we are in Christ, relying on the power of God. Oh, he can roar loudly and try to create fear. He can try to single us out like a lion does in nature, but when we resist and stand firmly; we create the ability to fight back. Lions in the Serengeti of Africa hide in the thick bush, waiting for their prey to search out a water source. If they try to cross the thick bush, the prey becomes breakfast, or a late night snack.

Most animals know that the lion is there. They actually stare at it, knowing that as long as they can see the lion, they are safe. It's when the lion cannot be seen that the danger is the greatest. So, be alert, and resist the enemy. Many of these animals will stay in groups for protection. You have heard, "There is strength in numbers." But if one of these animals wanders off, or is not paying attention to the movement of the "family," that is when they become a target, when they are separated and alone.

A word to the wise: stay alert, stay strong, resist him, and stand firmly in the faith. Stay together, watch each

Peter ONE

other's back, fight shoulder to shoulder defending the faith, and know that we are all in this together.

Don't separate yourself from the flock. Separation makes you an easy target. Stay, stand, fight, and win. Your brothers and sisters are standing with you. Stand steadfast in the faith, confide in God, and rely on Him alone. These are the cornerstones of resisting the enemy's lies, deception, and trouble.

God's strength is not diminished. His power is the greatest, and his love and grace will sustain us through any and all turmoil. We must only call on the name above all names: Jesus, our Lord. So, encourage each other with the knowledge of victory found in Christ alone! Stand strong. R – E – S – I – S - T the enemy.

5:10 And the God of all grace, who called you to his eternal glory in Christ, after you have suffered a little while, will himself restore you and make you strong, firm and steadfast.

I have grown to feel grace in my life. I rely on the grace of God for my next breath, and I give him thanks for my last one. My Father in Heaven loves us, and he has called us to his eternal glory in Christ. Will there be suffering here on Earth? Yes. Do we have everything we need to overcome it? Yes. God has called us into his eternal glory if we are saved, and we do not have to worry if he will leave us or forsake us once we are called. He said, *"I am with you always to the very end of the age"* (Matthew 28:20).

Peter ONE

He is with us to the end. Will we suffer? Yes, if he allows it. But our suffering here on Earth is short compared with eternity. The suffering is little when compared with eternal glory. The glory of God must be the focus, not the temporary suffering that he allows for our growth. If we can focus on the complete restoration that is in Christ Jesus, victory follows.

We live in a time when most people think it is unfair if they suffer at all. We live in a time when many people not only claim victim status, but also try to leverage being a victim for worldly gain. We are all victims. We can choose to complain that the suffering is hard, unfair, unjust, and unwanted, or we can be victims of love, grace, and growth, knowing that the trial is for only a short time.

We can be made weak in ourselves, or we can be made strong in Christ. We can let ourselves become soft in trials, or we can let trials and suffering produce strong resolve. We can let suffering wear us down until we feel like we want to give up, or we can trust our Lord to develop in us a strong, firm, and steadfast faith. We are free agents here on Earth, and we can decide whom we will serve this day. As for me and my house, we will serve the Lord.

These temporary sufferings in Christ make us who we are. They grow us. They create a perfect reliance on our God, and they help create a more perfect faith. The suffering you're going through now – please know that it is temporary. It is allowed by God to grow you,

Peter ONE

strengthen you, and build you into a more perfect follower of Jesus.

The firm foundation of our faith is not accomplished without some digging. We have to get to the bedrock of our soul in order that the foundation can be formed, poured, and reinforced by the Master Builder. Then, on this strong foundation, he will build you and I into what he had always planned for us. Remember, you have to go through the building process. I encourage you to enjoy even the hard parts!

5:11 To him be the power for ever and ever. Amen.

To God, and God alone, be the power. He is the power, holds the power, and confers the power to his children. He, and he alone, is worthy of our praise and honor. We say, "Amen," to an eternity of power found in Jehovah God.

Final Greetings

5:12 With the help of Silas, whom I regard as a faithful brother, I have written to you briefly, encouraging you and testifying that this is the true grace of God. Stand fast in it.

Peter is talking about his friend, Silas. It is the same Silas whom Paul mentions in 1 Thessalonians 1:1 and in 2 Corinthians 1:19. He is also mentioned in the Book of

Peter ONE

Acts as being with Paul (Acts 16:25). This guy was a committed follower of Christ, undoubtedly.

How he became acquainted with Peter, or why he was with him in Babylon, is anyone's guess. Let's just say that he knew how to network, and he seemed to be right where God needed him at the right time. Right time, right place. Silas was a faithful brother.

Peter encourages us to stand fast in the grace of God, to testify of his goodness and love whenever we are given the chance. We are to bear witness to the truth. Today, we are to walk in the truth, speak the truth, know that we are loved, and seek after the lost. I challenge you to allow the Living God to move you, equip you, strengthen you, and use you as an instrument of his glory.

5:13 She who is in Babylon, chosen together with you, sends you her greetings, and so does my son Mark.

Here, Babylon is not to be confused with the Babylon in Egypt, Jerusalem, or Rome. It is the actual place in Ancient Assyria. Most people agree that the "she" in this verse is the Church, but some maintain that the reference may be to a Christian woman, possibly to Peter's wife. If that is the case, then "she" would have been very well known throughout the region. Everyone should have been able to know whom Peter was referring to. The bottom line is that Peter, in his final

Peter ONE

thoughts, is saying that "she" is chosen, as were his audience was chosen, that would be us.

"My son Mark" is likely the same John Mark who is mentioned in Acts. He would be the same Mark who wrote the Gospel that goes by that name of "Mark." Of course, Mark was not Peter's biological son, but Peter probably had a part to play in his salvation. So, he is a spiritual son to Peter, and Peter refers to him in terms of affection.

Just a few short generations ago, when a man married the daughter of a family, he became another child to the parents of the bride. The celebration of marriage was to welcome the two families into a relationship that would produce future generations. It was a happy occasion. You didn't lose a daughter; instead, you gained a son. It is a term of endearment to be called "son," instead of son-in-law. It was a joy to gain another child.

5:14 Greet one another with a kiss of love.

Peace to all of you who are in Christ.

Ok, now you've gone too far. A kiss? Really? I mean, I don't even do that with the people I am close to. I can hear some of you now: "Hey, I am just getting used to the hugging thing. Man, I was proud of myself for moving past a handshake or a nod. But kiss? Are you out of your mind, Peter?"

Peter ONE

Remember that in many cultures, it is offensive to grab someone's hand, to squeeze it, and then to move it in an up-down motion. Something as simple as a handshake seems normal to us, but many around the world do not understand the meaning in the motion. It was the Quakers who made it a popular sign of equality under God. The "kiss" mentioned here by Peter was customary to Ancient Judea. Practiced by the early Church, it was a kiss of peace, a holy kiss, on the cheek. It was an embrace to show peace and friendship. Mentioned five times in the New Testament, this kiss was a common practice.

Then, there was the kiss of betrayal that Judas had arranged as a sign (Mark 14). He said, *"The one I kiss is the man; arrest him and lead him away under guard."*

Luke 22:47-48 reads as follows: *"While he was still speaking a crowd came up, and the man who was called Judas, one of the Twelve, was leading them. He approached Jesus to kiss him, but Jesus asked him, 'Judas, are you betraying the Son of Man with a kiss?'"*

One of the twelve, for 30 pieces of silver, betrayed our Savior with a kiss of peace. He signaled that this is the one to capture. He used what was considered a holy greeting to carry out a unholy plan. He later hung himself.

Yes, this "kiss" was a sign, and it had to be done for the salvation of all mankind. But what about now? How do

Peter ONE

we humans take holiness and turn it into unholy acts of betrayal?

With our words, we destroy friendships, families, and futures. With our greed, we grab 30 pieces of silver, missing the holy increase of God. We could have had something much more valuable than silver or gold. With bitter envy, we hold impure thoughts and harm against our brothers and sisters. With lust in our hearts, we settle for the crumbs of the world, while Jesus has prepared a feast for us.

We betray the faith every day that we choose to walk in our defeat and not in the victory found in Christ. We are called to a higher purpose, to a greater good. The high call of God is upon us. May we walk in this peace found in Christ.

In wrapping up his first epistle, Peter has encouraged us in peace. Remember, it had been several years since Simon Peter and the other eleven men called by Jesus had shared a meal together.

It is generally thought that Saint Peter died somewhere between AD 64 and 67. He spent a good deal of time spreading the gospel by word of mouth and deed. Then, he recorded some words for the ages. This fisherman from the village of Bethsaida, called Simon Peter, was called into ministry with his brother, Andrew, and they accomplished much.

Peter ONE

My encouragement: go fishing. You never know what God will speak to your heart. Peter was there. He saw the sick healed, he listened to the beatitudes, and he heard the first "Our Father" prayer from the mouth of Jesus.

He was challenged to go to the lost sheep of Israel. When asked by Jesus, "Who do you say I Am," his answer is an example of what our answer should be.

"Who do you say I Am," asked Jesus. Simon Peter answered, "You are the Christ, the Son of the Living God" (Matthew 16:16). So, Peter confessed Jesus as God's son, and he was blessed by God.

Today, confess Jesus as your Lord, and let the blessings of that flow from God's throne, flow into your heart and your life.

Peter saw the little children who were brought to Jesus, he saw Jesus place his hands on them, and he heard him say that the Kingdom of Heaven belongs to those with childlike faith.

My question is: do we make it too complicated? Do we come as children, or do we come with all of our "grown up" knowledge and problems? Peter heard the words spoken by Christ, he walked daily with the Lord, and, when it came to the end of Jesus's earthly ministry, Simon Peter denied Christ.

Peter ONE

Had he forgotten all the teachings and miracles he had witnessed? Had Peter forgotten that he walked on water, too? In Matthew 14:22-33, we read how Peter said to Jesus, *"Lord, if it's you... tell me to come to you on the water." Jesus said, "Come." Then, Peter got out of the boat, walked on the water, and came toward Jesus."*

We read, "But when he saw the wind he was afraid, and beginning to sink, he cried out, 'Lord, save me.'"

A picture of faith, Peter was the other guy that walked on water. A picture of fear, he started to sink. A picture of action, he said, "Lord, save me!"

At the end of the gospel accounts, we read that Peter disowns and denies Christ. We also read that, after the resurrection, Peter was reinstated by Jesus. He was one of many who were given the great commission, and he spent the rest of his life fulfilling it. He was crucified in Rome under Emperor Nero Augustus Caesar. He asked to be crucified upside down. He saw himself as unworthy to be crucified in the same way as Jesus Christ.

Peter lived the gamut of emotions. From fisherman to Disciple to Apostle he lived it full. From walking on water, to denying Christ and from denying Christ to becoming a voice of the Way, then dying for his faith. There is much to be taken from this first letter of Peter, and from a life lived as a follower of Christ.

Peter ONE

My hope and prayer is that we, too, learn to follow Christ. We can yell out, "Jesus, save me," when we are in trouble. We can finish strong, until the appointed time for us to meet Our Lord face to face.

May you walk through the storms of life trusting our Lord Jesus. And may you never ever forget that you are loved.   – **Amen**

Peter ONE

DEDICATED TO MY FATHER
GOD

Peter ONE

Other Titles by Mel Reed:
James & I & You: *A conversation with the Brother of Jesus.* This modern day commentary on the book of James allows you to have a seat at the table, have conversation like a close friend of James, and ponder the meaning of his words. (2013-Optimus Training)

Peter ONE: A modern day commentary on First Peter. Peter is "The other guy that walked on water!" Peter ONE, will help you embrace your position in Christ and challenge you to live in the center of Gods heart, even when all hell is trying to destroy your faith. (2014-Optimus Training)

365 MEN: *A daily QUEST for men.* Daily readings and prayer to equip men each day of the year. (2015-Optimus Training)

NFL-Never Fail Leadership: There are marks of true leadership all around us. Never Fail Leadership uncovers the truth about leadership and outlines how to take those timeless principals from the NFL and apply them to your business and family life. From the locker room, to the board room, to the living room, leadership matters.

MEL REED Has spent years in business and ministry making him uniquely qualified for creating leadership God's way. A Graduate of Colorado Christian University, Mel is President of RealMen Ministries, Inc. and Optimus Training Corporation, LLC.

Mel Reed is available to speak at your next event. To book Mel please visit: **OptimusTraining.com~479-957-3307**

www.ingramcontent.com/pod-product-compliance
Lightning Source LLC
Chambersburg PA
CBHW051651040426
42446CB00009B/1080